Themes

An integrated skills course for late intermediate and advanced students

Alan Matthews and Carol Read

Collins ELT

For Joey and Jozef

© Alan Matthews and Carol Read

First published 1982
Reprinted 1982,
1983, 84, 85 (twice), 87, 88

7 8 9 10

All rights reserved. No part of this book may be
reproduced, stored in a retrieval system, or
transmitted in any form or by any means,
electronic, mechanical, photocopying,
recording or otherwise, without the prior
permission in writing of the Publisher.

Collins ELT
8 Grafton Street
London W1X 3LA
Printed in Great Britain by Scotprint Ltd, Musselburgh

ISBN 0 00 370040 2

This book is accompanied by a cassette

We are grateful to the following for permission to reproduce or make use of copyright material:

Unit 2 — *Living Well*, p. 15, ed. Tresidder, J., Mitchell Beazley 1977
Unit 6 — Rupert Crewe Ltd (horoscopes) from the ORION Astrological forecasts published in the *Daily Mail*, 17 February 1982
Unit 8 — London Link-up Club (advertisement)
Unit 9 — *Connexions*, 'Out of Your Mind', © Peter Newmark, 1968, 1972, 1977, Penguin Education
Unit 10 — *Time Out*, *The Times* (advertisements)
Unit 13 — *New Society*, April 1980 ('Travel to Work')
Unit 14 — 'Britain's Sixteen-Year-Olds', ed. Fogelman, K. National Children's Bureau 1976
Unit 15 — Adapted from 'Whales' and 'Whaling' in *Encyclopaedia Britannica*, 15th edition (1974), by permission of Encyclopaedia Britannica, Inc; Friends of the Earth (article and chart)
Unit 16 — *The Times*, *The Daily Mail* (London), *The Sun* (articles about smallpox report and 'Bra girl')
Unit 19 — *Now*! magazine, 22 February 1980 ('Watching with Mother')
Unit 20 — *Connexions*, 'Break for Commercials', © Edith Rudinger and Vic Kelly, 1970, Penguin Education
Unit 21 — 1. *Design for Today*, Schools Council Design and Craft Education Project, © Schools Council Publications 1974
2. British Code of Advertising Practice Committee (General Principles)
Unit 26 — *Time Out*, March 28–April 3 1980, ('Staying Alive' and 'Commuting by Bicycle')
Unit 27 — *Living Well*, op. cit.
Unit 28 — 1. *Summerhill: A Radical Approach to Child Rearing* by A. S. Neill, © 1960 Hart Publishing Co.
2. *Guardian Weekly*, June/July 1979 ('Learning in the School of Life') Pat Rowe
Unit 29 — *The Times*, 4 March 1980 (article and editorial)
Unit 30 — 1. *High Life* magazine, British Airways, December 1979 ('Who's Afraid of the Silicon Chip?')
2. *Observer* magazine, 18 November 1979 (illustration reference for 'Today's Town')

Contents

	page
General Introduction	v
Teacher's Notes	vi

You and Other People

1 First Impressions	14
2 Body Shapes and Behaviour	17
3 Friend of a Friend Ⓣ	22
4 Posture	24
5 Faces Ⓣ	26
6 Elemental Truths	28
7 Doodling	31
8 Making New Friends	33

You and Your Environment

9 Give Us Our Daily Drugs	36
10 Sharing a Home	39
11 Housing Ⓣ	43
12 Your Neighbourhood	45
13 Travel to Work	47
14 Teenagers' Leisure and Pleasure Ⓣ	51
15 How Much Do You Know about Whales?	54

You and the Media

16 What the Papers Said	60
17 A Foreign Correspondent Ⓣ	66
18 The Soap Opera	69
19 Children and Television Ⓣ	71
20 The Language of Advertising	75
21 Consumer Discrimination	78
22 A Change Is as Good as a Rest Ⓣ	81

You and Alternatives

23 Is Being Single Still out of Line?	86
24 Living Collectively Ⓣ	91
25 Getting Away from It All Ⓣ	93
26 The Pneu Wave	96
27 Vegetarianism	101
28 Schools with a Difference	106
29 Super Race?	111
30 Who's Afraid of the Silicon Chip? Ⓣ	115

Oral Functions Bank
Reference Grid   122
Exponents and Practice Exercises

1 Asking for and Giving Opinions   124
2 Explaining and Justifying   126
3 Asking for and Giving Clarification   127
4 Expressing Agreement and Disagreement   129
5 Interrupting   131
6 Describing People   132
7 Introducing Oneself and Giving Personal Information   133
8 Talking about Likes and Interests   134
9 Expressing Preferences   136
10 Making Complaints   137
11 Giving Warnings   138
12 Asking for and Giving Advice   139
13 Asking for More Detailed Information   141
14 Making and Responding to Suggestions   142
15 Making Plans and Proposals   144
16 Talking in Favour of or Against a Proposal   145
17 Making Predictions   147
18 Expressing Degrees of Certainty and Uncertainty   148
19 Making Comparisons   149
20 Making Generalisations   150

Gapped Tapescripts   152

Answer Key   166

Authors' Acknowledgements

We would like to thank the following people for their assistance in the production of these materials: Mike Beaumont, Frank Frankel, Hania Januriek, Bob Jordan, Melinda Mourão, Teresa O' Brien and Alan Reditt for their help with recording; Terry McMylor and Heather Branwell for their technical help in recording and editing the tapes; Teresa Nunes da Silva and Edith Foerster for typing the draft manuscript. We are also grateful to Bob Jordan for all his suggestions, comments and advice and to Gordon Jarvie, Sheila Ferguson and Sarah Thorpe for being such cooperative and understanding editors.

Finally, the materials in 'Themes' have been developed and tried out in the British Institute, Lisbon, Portugal and we would like to thank all the teachers and students who piloted them and gave us many useful comments and suggestions.

General Introduction

What Is 'Themes'?

'Themes' is a collection of lively, stimulating teaching materials suitable for late intermediate and advanced learners of English who wish to develop their ability in listening, speaking, reading and writing to a high level of proficiency. The materials are all based on authentic texts — newspaper articles, charts, tables, interviews, etc. The aim is to provide the learner with motivating practice incorporating the four skills within a naturally integrated framework.

The book is organised into four main sections, each of which is based on a broad thematic area such as 'You and Other People' and 'You and Your Environment'. Each section is subdivided into seven or eight units containing varied, topical textual material. The accompanying activities — which often require the students to write answers or make notes in the spaces provided — include a wide range of up-to-date methodological techniques in the teaching of English to advanced students. In all there are thirty units. It is not intended that these units be worked through one after the other but rather that the teacher covers them in the order he/she thinks best according to the interests of the students and the syllabus they are following.

A special feature of 'Themes' is the *Oral Functions Bank* at the back of the book. It is expected that the students already possess a fairly good grasp of English grammar and perhaps also some familiarity with the main exponents of the most common language functions. 'Themes' aims to activate this knowledge but it is recognised that in order to do this successfully it may well be necessary to give the students initial, more controlled practice in expressing the main functions which occur in any given unit. The *Oral Functions Bank* serves this purpose. Exponents of the main functions occurring in each unit are listed with an indication of their relative formality; controlled language exercises provide the students with the opportunity to practise handling the exponents correctly and appropriately.

'Themes' also includes a tape of listening material (available on cassette) which forms an integral part of ten of the units. The tapescripts at the back of the book are gapped in order to provide further practice in intensive listening. A full answer key is also included.

The symbol Ⓣ indicates recorded material.

The symbol Ⓚ indicates those exercises for which there are answers in the Answer Key.

Who Is 'Themes' for?

The teaching material in 'Themes' has been prepared for late intermediate and advanced students of any nationality who are:

- *(i)* preparing for the University of Cambridge 'Certificate of Proficiency in English', or an equivalent public examination;
- *(ii)* following an advanced English language course at secondary school or university;
- *(iii)* doing a short intensive or semi-intensive course either in their own country or in an English-speaking country.

- 'Themes' assumes that the students already have a broad structural knowledge of English roughly at the level of the University of Cambridge 'First Certificate in English'.
- 'Themes' does not give explicit training in examination technique but provides the students with adult, topical and motivating frameworks for the development of their language skills up to the level required by an examination such as the Cambridge 'Proficiency'.
- 'Themes' is designed especially for use with groups of approximately ten or more students — it is not intended as self-access material.

Aims of 'Themes'

- to develop students' ability in the four skills in an integrated way but with a special focus on speaking. Reading and listening texts are normally lead-ins to communicative oral/aural activities. Suggestions for written tasks are given where they form realistic extensions of the preceding activities;
- to provide interesting, relevant and topical materials which will encourage the students to think and to participate in class activities and express their personal opinions;
- to guide learners in the appropriate use of different exponents of major language functions;
- to extend and enrich students' active vocabulary.

Teacher's Notes

Introduction

'Themes' is especially designed to be used with classes of ten or more students. Group work and discussion-type activities, which feature regularly throughout the materials, are more successful with at least this number. 'Themes' can also be used with larger classes: the frequent organisation of students into groups and pairs means that all students are active and involved all the time and opportunities for language practice are maximised.

The materials in 'Themes' are designed on the principle of 'cooperative learning': students are usually asked initially to attempt a task on their own, but in the next stage they check and compare their answers with another student or group of students. During this time, there is opportunity for a great deal of valuable language practice: students help each other, check their answers together, disagree about their answers, justify and explain the differences, persuade each other they are right, etc. By the time the whole class discusses the task, the students have probably been able, through a cooperative effort, to work out the answers for themselves. The teacher can confirm whether these are right and help to resolve any difficulties that may have arisen. We have found that students at this level find it both motivating and useful to work in this way. It provides a framework for extensive language practice and interaction among all the members of a class and also fosters an atmosphere where learners not only look to the teacher, but to each other, for help and guidance in carrying out tasks and resolving language difficulties.

In 'Themes' none of the units has exactly the same format, although they do all follow the same general pattern. A listening and/or reading text forms the basis of each unit and, after a variety of tasks and vocabulary exercises, leads into some kind of speaking activity, for example, a role-play. This, in turn, provides the preparation for a writing task, such as a letter or report. There are two main reasons for maintaining a different format for each unit. Firstly, the format and design of each unit has been determined by the nature of the materials selected. Secondly, we feel that a varied format makes 'Themes' more intrinsically interesting to use both for student and teacher alike.

Learner-centred Activities and the Role of the Teacher

In 'Themes' there is a combination of familiar listening and reading tasks as well as a range of more learner-centred activities. For parts of each unit students work independently of the teacher either in pairs or small groups. The activities they are asked to do range from checking textual comprehension and working out the meaning of vocabulary to preparing for role-play, planning campaigns and designing a house. There are many advantages in working in pairs or small groups in this way:

- Everyone in the class is working simultaneously and therefore each student performs more frequently;
- Students can work at their own pace rather than at a pace which is imposed;
- Students are encouraged to be personally involved and to take initiative in the learning process. This is more motivating and often more fun;
- The teacher can move from group to group listening to the work of individual students.

Whenever class organisation is learner-centred, the teacher is able to move around the class freely and play a variety of different roles:

- To give individual help to less able students;
- To be a source of information, *eg.* answering queries about grammar and vocabulary;
- To encourage students and give suggestions, ideas and advice, if necessary;
- To listen and make a note of recurring errors for subsequent remedial treatment.

It is important, however, that the teacher should be as unobtrusive as possible in all these roles. The teacher is there to help if and when help is required, but for the most part the students are working by themselves.

The Oral Functions Bank

The Oral Functions Bank provides language input to each of the units in 'Themes' to be used at the discretion of the teacher and according to the needs of the students. The Oral Functions Bank is intended to be used for oral work only, although many of the language exponents given are also appropriate in the written medium. For each major language function a selection of exponents is given to cover a range from informal to formal. The degree of formality of each exponent is indicated by a scale at the side of each language table. The selection of

vii

exponents for each language function is not meant to be comprehensive and the teacher should feel free to add to the given list if he/she thinks that this may be desirable.

Most of the language in the Oral Functions Bank will probably not be new to students of this level. However, it is often the case that although students may recognise the language exponents, they do not incorporate them naturally into their own language performance and have no clear idea of when to use them appropriately. The Oral Functions Bank is designed to remind the students of the exponents and to give them opportunity to practise using them, before moving on to the unit in 'Themes' in which they are likely to occur. The formality scale is designed to increase the students' awareness of the appropriacy of different language exponents in different situations.

There are two sets of practice exercises given for each of the major language functions in the Oral Functions Bank. The first set is more controlled and based on a series of cued exchanges. The second set is freer and the students are usually required to produce language exponents that are appropriate to a specific situation given in the exercise. The exercises may be done either with the teacher, or, after one or two examples have been given, in pairs.

Recommended Procedure for Using a Unit of 'Themes'

1 Select the unit that you want to do with your class;
2 Consult the Oral Functions Bank grid on p. 122 to see what major language functions occur in the unit you have chosen;
3 Decide which Oral Functions Bank exercises, if any, you think your students need to do before starting the unit;
4 Look through the unit itself. Familiarise yourself with the content and decide on any vocabulary you need to pre-teach. This is probably best integrated into the 'warm-up' to the theme;
5 Do the activities of the unit in sequence with your class following the detailed instructions given.

Activity-types in 'Themes'

Below is a brief description of the main kinds of activities included in 'Themes' and some suggestions on how best to use them.

NB. Each activity-type is not necessarily found in each unit.

Listening Activities

These form a central component of ten of the units in 'Themes'. All the texts are based on either semi-scripted or unscripted dialogues, interviews, telephone conversations and descriptions. Tasks include note-taking, information transfer and exercises based on the students making predictions about what they are going to hear on the tape.

Before doing a listening activity with your students it is important to orient them to the text and to the task you want them to do. For this purpose pre-listening activities, which may be either a discussion or an initial task, are included in each of the relevant units.

It is important to give the students plenty of opportunity to listen. If they do not follow the text at first, be ready to play it again. Make sure however that the time

viii

spent listening is always purposeful, ie. that the students always have a set task to do while listening to the tape.

All the listening activities are suitable for use either with a tape-recorder and the whole class working together, or for work in the language laboratory with individual students working at their own pace. If the listening activity is done in the classroom it is a good idea to get students to do the tasks on their own initially and then to check their answers in pairs before listening to the tape again, if this is found to be necessary, and going through the answers to the task with the whole class.

For optional additional, intensive listening practice, you can ask the students to listen to all or part of the text again and complete the gapped tapescripts on pp. 152–165. The main focus here is on the understanding and identification of contracted verb forms, *eg. 'we're* prepared...' and *'there's* got to be...' and weak form usage, *eg. 'for* a couple *of* years' and *'can* set up *his* own ...'. A key to the exercises is on p. 166.

Reading Activities

Reading passages, taken from a wide variety of authentic sources such as newspapers, magazines, books and reports, form the basis of many of the units in 'Themes'. Tasks include note-taking, information transfer, and matching exercises as well as tasks which require the students to pick out the main ideas in a text, and to evaluate its style and content critically.

All the texts used in 'Themes' are meant to be read silently by the students. Before the students begin reading, it is important to orient them to the contents and style of the text. Orientation activities, such as pre-discussion questions, and prediction exercises are usually included in the unit for this purpose. The students are normally required to read the text more than once. In the first reading, the set task requires the students to read for gist or to find specific information. It may be a good idea to give a time limit for this — it can be motivating and helps to develop the students' reading speed as well as their accuracy.

During the second reading of the text, the students may be asked to perform a more extended task, such as completing an information transfer or guided notes. It is a good idea to get the students to work individually at first and then to check their answers in pairs, before going through the task with the whole class. The check stage of the task provides valuable opportunity for language practice. You should encourage the students to discuss their answers as far as possible and to refer back to the text where they disagree.

It is important to remember that students are likely to have different reading speeds and that you may need to make allowances for this. It is also a good idea to encourage students who work more quickly to help slower and less able students at the check stage.

Vocabulary Exercises

These are not automatically included after every Listening and Reading text in 'Themes', but only where they seem to be necessary or useful to the learners. There are a variety of exercise types used including matching words/phrases with definitions, labelling diagrams, working out meanings from contextual clues and choosing appropriate definitions from a given list.

The vocabulary exercises are best done individually and you should make sure that the students always refer back to the context in which the word or phrase occurs. The students can then check and compare their answers in pairs before the teacher confirms the right ones. The teacher should avoid working through the vocabulary exercises too quickly and should be alert to the potential discussion possibilities that students' different interpretations may give rise to.

Role-play Activities
These are included in a number of the units in 'Themes', and usually follow on from an earlier reading or listening task. They may involve the students working in pairs, small groups or with the whole class together. The role-plays vary from relatively controlled, where a model is provided in the preceding listening activity, to much freer, where students develop their own ideas in response to a given situation or piece of information.

A successful role-play depends on the students being given enough time for preparation. It may be a good idea to set a time limit, so that they know exactly how long they have got. During the preparation stage, the teacher should be available to answer queries and to give help in the expression of the students' own ideas. The teacher should also be ready to offer ideas and suggestions to less imaginative students, if this seems necessary.

It is important that during the role-play itself the teacher's presence is unobtrusive and he or she does not interrupt to correct the students. It is a good idea, however, to note down any major errors that occur; these may be pointed out at the end of the role-play or used as the basis for future remedial work.

The length of class time allotted to the role-play obviously depends on the content and the group of students who have prepared it and is, therefore, best left to the teacher's discretion. You may find, however, that it is a good idea to give a time limit, at least in role-plays such as formal meetings, where this seems appropriate.

Class Discussions
These are usually included either at the beginning of a unit as part of the introduction and orientation to the theme, or as a follow-up to pair and group work when students report back and discuss with the whole class a task they have just done.

The teacher can either appoint a student to informally chair the discussion or do this him/herself. The teacher should adopt a low-profile role in class discussions, but it is important to make sure that everyone has a chance to speak. Class discussions will obviously vary in length but it is always a good idea to bring them to a close before anyone begins to lose interest.

Pair and Group Work
Pair and group work activities are included in every unit. The students are asked to perform a whole range of tasks which include interpreting pictures, designing a home, doing quizzes, working out the plot for a TV serial and many more. The main point of organising the students to work in pairs and groups is that, like this, every student is given maximum opportunity to play an active listening and speaking part. It is a good idea to vary the pairs and groups of students working

together from unit to unit. Remember also to bear in mind the personalities and abilities of the students when you divide them up into pairs and groups.

Writing Activities

These are included at the end of every unit; occasionally there is a writing activity earlier in the unit as well. All the writing activities are natural and appropriate extensions of earlier tasks. They include letters, reports, descriptions, dialogues and newspaper articles as well parallel and summary writing exercises.

Although 'Themes' does not explicitly aim to teach writing skills, the activities suggested provide a contextualised framework in which to practise writing and thereby consolidate other work which has been done in the unit. The writing activities are placed at the end of each unit so that they can be prepared for by earlier activities. By the time the students are asked to write, they have the necessary vocabulary and ideas at their disposal to enable them to do the task successfully.

The writing activities in 'Themes' can either be done for homework or in class.

You and Other People

1	**First Impressions**	*page* 14
2	**Body Shapes and Behaviour**	17
3	**Friend of a Friend** Ⓣ	22
4	**Posture**	24
5	**Faces** Ⓣ	26
6	**Elemental Truths**	28
7	**Doodling**	31
8	**Making New Friends**	33

Unit 1 First Impressions

A1 When we meet someone for the first time, we inevitably form an opinion about what that person is like, even though this may change on further acquaintance.

Which features do you notice most when you meet someone for the first time? Do you notice the same features for a man as for a woman?

2 Look at the list below and mark the 3 features you notice most:
- *(a)* in a woman.
- *(b)* in a man.

Are there any features omitted from the list below? Add them in the spaces provided.

Feature	Woman	Man
Height		
Build		
Colour of hair		
Colour of eyes		
Facial features		
Facial expressions		
Nervous mannerisms		
Gestures		
Shape of hands		
Dress		
Accessories, *eg.* jewellery, make-up		
Voice		
Posture, *eg.* hunched shoulders, straight back		

3 Compare your choices with your partner's and explain your reasons for selecting them.
4 Listen to the opinions of other students and see how far you agree with them. Is there any difference between the opinions of the male students and female students in your class? Discuss the reasons why this might be so.

Ⓚ **B Vocabulary**
How accurately can you describe someone?

1 *Facial Features*
Look at the drawing of a face below and label as many of the features as you can.

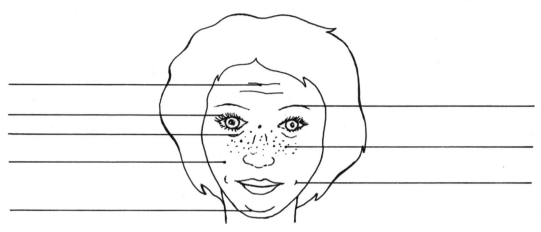

Compare your work with your partner's. Help each other to complete the labelling correctly, if necessary.

2 *Hair*
(i) Look at the ways of describing different hair colours below. Explain the colour meant by each. *Eg.* blonde—very light-coloured hair.
    (a) Auburn—   *(d)* Chestnut-coloured—
    (b) Sandy—   *(e)* Greying—
    (c) Mousey—   *(f)* Fair—

(ii) Match the following adjectives correctly with the pictures below. Write the appropriate letter in the box.
    (a) curly   *(b)* straight   *(c)* wavy   *(d)* frizzy

3 *Build*

(i) The following words have a similar meaning to *thin*:

    (a) slim   *(b)* slender   *(c)* skinny   *(d)* slight

If used in a description, which of the words suggests that the person is

    (i) *too* thin _____

    (ii) also frail _____

    (iii) also graceful _____

    (iv) thin but *not* too thin _____

(ii) The following words have a similar meaning to *fat*:

    (a) plump   *(b)* podgy   *(c)* stout   *(d)* thick-set

If used in a description, which of the words suggests that the person

    (i) is also strong and resilient _____

    (ii) is fat in a pleasant way _____

    (iii) is short and solidly built _____

    (iv) could easily lose weight _____

C   Divide into pairs and sit back to back. Note down the features you can most clearly remember about your partner. Without turning round tell each other what these are and see how accurate you have been.

D **Writing**

Write a letter to a friend giving your first impressions of *either* a fellow student *or* someone you have recently met.

Unit 2 Body Shapes and Behaviour

A1 An American psychologist, William Sheldon, devised a useful system of categorizing people in 1940. He defined three basic body types—the endomorph, the mesomorph and the ectomorph.

The endomorph is rounded, heavily built and with quite a lot of fat (though not necessarily obese). The mesomorph is the classic, well-muscled athlete. The ectomorph is thin and angular, with not much muscle and not much fat.

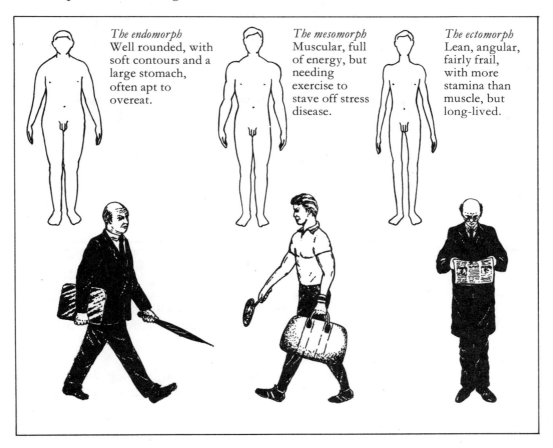

The endomorph
Well rounded, with soft contours and a large stomach, often apt to overeat.

The mesomorph
Muscular, full of energy, but needing exercise to stave off stress disease.

The ectomorph
Lean, angular, fairly frail, with more stamina than muscle, but long-lived.

Sheldon's description is of basic body shape and it stands regardless of what you weigh and how fat you may be. A fat ectomorph is not an endomorph — he is a fat ectomorph who should lose some weight.

Whatever shape you were born with, you can be physically fit, but what you need to do to achieve fitness will be dictated by your shape. Extreme mesomorphs need a lot of exercise — much more than extreme examples of the other types. Endomorphs and ectomorphs should not strain to match mesomorphs in sport. Where they can succeed is in sports that require skill and practice: fencing, tennis, squash. Ectomorphs for all their lack of strength, have the great advantage that their health is normally the best. By the same token, the stressed mesomorph is often in the worst position.

ⓚ **2** Using the information and illustrations on p. 17 classify the following body shapes:—

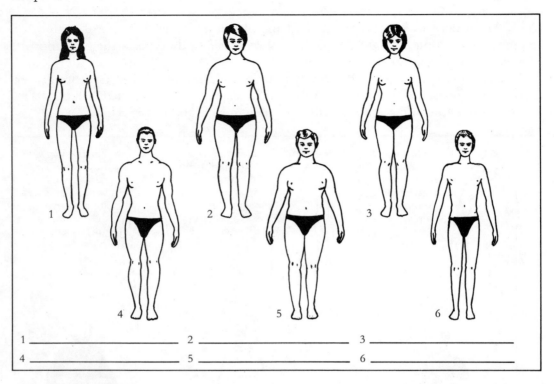

1 _____ 2 _____ 3 _____
4 _____ 5 _____ 6 _____

3 Which shape do you prefer
   (a) in a woman? ☐   *(b)* in a man? ☐
4 Discuss your choices first with your partner and then with the rest of the class.
5 Do they correspond with the findings of the Consumers' Association below?

> *The Favourite Body*
> The Adman's ideal physique is usually the tall, lean type with broad shoulders and narrow hips. In 1971 the Consumers' Association organised a survey in Britain which largely confirmed the popularity of this meso-ecto-morphic shape. But many people, particularly the middle-aged, prefer a more endomorphic version. A range of 6 average body shapes of equal heights was offered for each sex and people asked which they liked best. Whereas 1 was the favourite female shape, some middle-aged women liked 2, as did many older men. Third favourite was 3. Of the male shapes, 4 was much the most popular with women and was also the favourite with men, followed by 5. Many young women preferred 6, but fewer men.

ⓚ **B1** Human behaviour is more influenced by basic body shape than might be thought. Each body type has certain associated behaviour patterns, though the link is far from hard and fast. Personality is obviously more complicated than the shape of arms, legs or torso.

Below are descriptions of the characteristic behaviour of each of the three different body types. Read them and match each of the adjectives below with the correct body type. Write your answers in the boxes provided.

complacent   controlled   dominant

aggressive   tolerant   responsive

Endomorphs		Mesomorphs		Ectomorphs

Endomorphs are marked above all by being relaxed. Their whole body, action and life-style are affected. As the features are rounded, so the movement of the body is smooth and deliberate. The endomorph reacts slowly, and there is a strong element of complacency, a tendency to make the best of any situation regardless of the future. At times this can appear to others as infuriating indifference. The other side of the coin is tolerance, an acceptance of people, customs and situations. This means that endomorphs are usually companionable.

Mesomorphs normally have a commanding stance, with the shoulders back and head up. Everything gives the appearance of readiness for action. The mesomorph often has a deep and abiding desire to dominate, to be important, to wield power. When on a winning streak this trait can manifest itself in expansiveness and generosity. When difficulties arise however, the mesomorph seeks refuge in action. The marked mesomorph tends to be highly competitive and abounds in drive and enterprise. He is aggressive and often a dare-devil and a gambler too.

The typical *ectomorph*, slender and sensitive, is extremely responsive to everything that goes on around him. He tends to be fussy about his diet and his sensitivity to pain makes him something of a hypochondriac. The ectomorph is usually a highly-controlled person. He has sharp eyes and ears and his reactions are very fast. His posture is often tense and his movements unspontaneous. In conversation the ectomorph may appear ambiguous, hesitant or withdrawn when in fact he is probably more aware of events than everyone else. In times of crisis he is likely to seek solitude. The ectomorph tends to do well in intelligence tests and exams and to be quick to absorb new information.

2   Check and compare your answers with your partner.

Ⓚ   **C   Vocabulary**

Work out the meaning of the following from the context in which they are used above:

(i)   the other side of the coin   *(iii)*   on a winning streak

(ii)   a commanding stance   *(iv)*   abounds in drive and enterprise

D1 Look at the pictures of the four famous personalities below. Try to classify them according to the descriptions you have read. Write your answers in the spaces below the photographs.

(i) _____   (ii) _____

(iii) _____   (iv) _____

2 Discuss your opinions first with your partner and then with the rest of the class. How far do you all agree? Is it valid to classify people in this way or is it too far-fetched?

E Writing

Look at the three photos below. Choose one and write a character sketch based on what you can surmise from the person's appearance.

(i)

(ii)

(iii)

Unit 3   Friend of a Friend

A1   Usually the way someone speaks is just one of many features on which we base our first impressions. But how much does it reveal of a person's character when it is the only thing we have to go by?

Here is a list of adjectives which are commonly used to describe people's characters. Decide whether each is *normally* used to describe:

  (i)   a positive feature;
  (ii)   a negative feature;
  (iii)   either, depending on the context.

superior	hesitant	confident	helpful
shy	cold	friendly	easygoing
warm	domineering	suspicious	aggressive
sensitive	wary	offputting	relaxed
understanding	neurotic	nervous	overbearing
indifferent			

Write each word in one of the appropriate columns below. The first three have been done for you. You might need to use a dictionary to help you.

Positive Feature	Negative Feature	Depending on the Context
warm	superior	shy

2   Compare and check what you have written first with your partner and then with the whole class. Discuss how far you all agree.

B1   You are now going to listen to three telephone conversations on the tape. A young man, Terry Jordan, has just arrived in England after hitch-hiking his way overland from Australia. Bill Evans, a friend of his who now lives in Sydney, has given him the phone numbers of three people to contact while he is in London. Terry hopes that they will agree to put him up.

22

As you listen to the conversations write down in the first column which, if any, of the adjectives discussed in **A** above fit your first impressions of the characters of the three people the hitch-hiker phones. If you wish, add any other suitable adjectives of your own.

Speaker	Adjectives	Reasons for Choice
Cathy O'Brien		
Norman Bowes		
Jan Simpson		

2 Now spend a moment thinking about the three phone conversations and note briefly the reason(s) for your choice of adjective(s) in the column provided.

3 Compare your choice of adjectives and impressions of each speaker with those of your partner. Do you agree with each other? What are the opinions of the rest of the class?

Ⓣ   Ⓚ   **C1**   Now listen to each phone conversation again and complete the table below.

Speaker	Connection with Bill Evans	Problems of staying (if any)	Outcome of phone call
Cathy O'Brien			
Norman Bowes			
Jan Simpson			

2 Compare and check your answers first with your partner and then with the whole class.

D Role-play

Work in pairs. Student A should imagine he/she is a hitch-hiker who arrives at the house of Student B and would like to be put up. Student A doesn't know Student B but is a friend of a friend. Hold the conversation.

E Writing

Write a dialogue between yourself and a friend of a friend who phones you up unexpectedly and asks whether he/she can stay with you for several weeks.

Unit 4 Posture

A1 Posture is an important means of conveying interpersonal attitudes. Postures are also associated with emotional states, either through direct physiological effects of emotions, or for symbolic reasons. Posture accompanies speech, in a way similar to that of gesture, though more slow-moving. There are powerful social conventions about the postures which are proper in a particular culture and in a particular situation.

Look at the different postures illustrated by the stick figures below and note down in the spaces provided any words or phrases which describe the attitudes you think they convey.

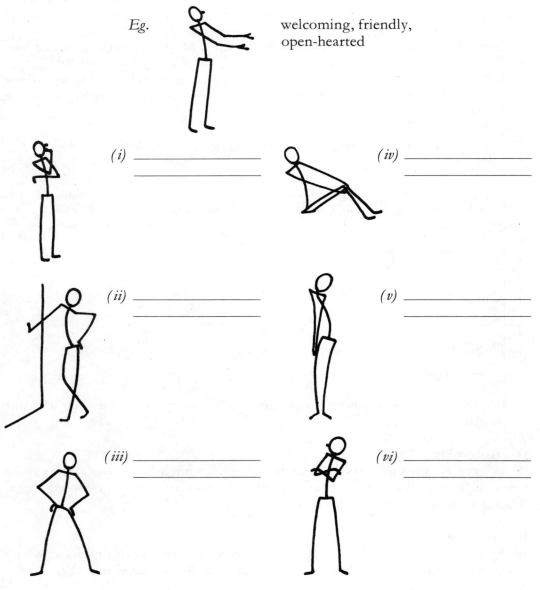

Eg. welcoming, friendly, open-hearted

(i) _____

(ii) _____

(iii) _____

(iv) _____

(v) _____

(vi) _____

2 Compare your interpretations of the figures first with your partner and then with the rest of the class.

B 1 Discuss with your partner which of the postures above you might expect the speakers to adopt in the following situations. Write the appropriate numbers in the boxes:

    1 A job applicant attending an interview. ☐

    2 A boss dismissing an employee. ☐

    3 A teenager at a party. ☐

    4 A lecturer giving a talk. ☐

    5 An owner showing people round his new house. ☐

    6 A father telling off his child. ☐

2 Now get together with another pair of students and compare your choices.

C Here are 4 more postures. In pairs:-
    (i) Decide which attitudes you think they convey.
    (ii) Suggest situations in which you might expect people to adopt them.

(i)   *(ii)*   *(iii)*   *(iv)*

D Writing

Choose any two of the figures in **C** above. Invent a situation and write a dialogue between them.

Unit 5 Faces

A1 Although we may notice many details about people's facial features they are often very difficult to describe in a distinctly recognisable way.

Listen to the four descriptions on the tape and match them with four of the pictures below. Write *(a)*, *(b)*, etc. in the spaces provided below the pictures:-

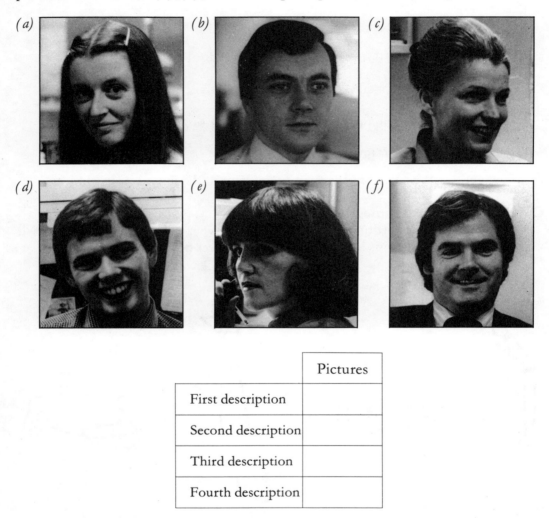

	Pictures
First description	
Second description	
Third description	
Fourth description	

2 Check and compare your answers with your partner. If necessary listen to the tape again.

3 Explain the reasons for your choices and discuss any differences of opinion with the whole class.

B1 Listen to the tape again and complete the table on the next page. Some of the information is already given to you. A cross (×) indicates that the information is not given on the tape. (NB. Before you start write the letter corresponding to each of the pictures in the space provided.)

	First Description (Picture ____)	Second Description (Picture ____)	Third Description (Picture ____)	Fourth Description (Picture ____)
Eyes	×	dark and lively		
Nose			not very large; rather broad	×
Mouth/Lips	small thin lips	×	×	rather thin lips
Hair		fairly dark		
Overall appearance	not very striking; fresh-faced		friendly and confident; over-confident?	attractive; rather angular
Build			stocky; rather overweight	
Personality	self-effacing; serious and reliable; fairly naive			kind and reserved; not easy to know; good, reliable friend
Hobbies/ Interests		parties; fast cars		

2 Compare and check what you have written with your partner. If necessary, listen to the tape again.

3 Do you think that the speakers' descriptions are accurate? Would you describe the people differently?

C Writing

1 Work in pairs. Look carefully at the two pictures which were *not* described. Using the headings in the table above (eyes, nose, etc.) make similar notes. Then write a description of these two people based on the other descriptions you heard on the tape.

2 Choose someone in the room and write a short paragraph describing his/her facial features as accurately as possible.

Either read out your description and see if the others can identify who you described.

Or get everyone to number his/her description. Pass them round the class and match them to the people described.

Unit 6 Elemental Truths

A1 We all belong to one of the four elements — Fire, Earth, Air or Water — depending on our date of birth. Look at the following table and see which one you belong to:-

Fire	Earth	Air	Water

Aries
  March 21–
  April 20
Leo
  July 22–
  August 21
Sagittarius
  November 23–
  December 20
	Capricorn
	  December 21–
	  January 19
	Taurus
	  April 21–
	  May 20
	Virgo
	  August 22–
	  September 22
		Aquarius
		  January 20–
		  February 18
		Gemini
		  May 21–
		  June 20
		Libra
		  September 23–
		  October 22
			Cancer
			  June 21–
			  July 21
			Scorpio
			  October 23–
			  November 22
			Pisces
			  February 19–
			  March 20

Ⓚ **2** Listed below are the principal characteristics ascribed to each element. Look at each set of characteristics in turn and do the vocabulary exercise which follows.

I

Pluses	Minuses
Good at decision making	Scatty
Dynamic	Bossy
Congenial	Superficial
Knowledgeable	Opinionated
Cheerful and optimistic	Cross and insensitive
Courageous	Foolhardy
Enthusiastic	Impetuous
Magnetic	Flirtatious

II

Pluses	Minuses
Sensitive and sympathetic	Moody and irritable at times
Co-operative	Evasive and elusive
Protective and calm	Turbulent and melodramatic
Idealistic	Pessimistic
Creative and artistic	Lazy and impractical
Inspiring to others	Dreamy and dopey
Long-suffering	Spineless

III

Pluses	Minuses
Practical and reliable	Dull and unimaginative
Staying within your income	Penny-pinching
Not expecting too much of life	Pessimistic
Consistent and persistent	Obstinate and stubborn
Hard-working	Unrelenting with self and others
Supportive and protective	Unsympathetic

IV

Pluses	Minuses
Sensible and objective	Smug
Co-operative and charming	Two-faced
Self-confident	Opinionated
Adaptable and willing	Superficially adaptable and willing
Good conversationalist	Over-talkative
Detached and reasonable	Cold and calculating
Lover of liberty	Lover of licence

Find words that have a similar meaning to the following in each set of characteristics:

In I   *(i)* disorganised and forgetful
          (ii) gets on easily with other people
          (iii) dogmatic in his/her ideas
          (iv) delights in needless risks

In II   *(v)* puts up with a lot without complaining
          (vi) sometimes feels sullen and gloomy
          (vii) slow; as if drugged
          (viii) lacks energy or resolution

In III   *(ix)* always gives help and backing
          (x) always on the look out for ways to economise

In IV   *(xi)* consciously self-satisfied
          (xii) insincere

3   Compare and check your answers with your partner.

Ⓚ   **B1**   Look at the four sets of characteristics again. Decide which of them you would associate with each different element. In order to do this, it may help to think of the personalities of friends and relatives whose birth dates you know.

    Write the appropriate number in each of the boxes:

    Fire ☐   Earth ☐   Air ☐   Water ☐

2   Compare your answers with your partner. Explain your choices and discuss any differences of opinion you have. How many of the characteristics ascribed to your element would you accept as accurate and apt?

C Writing

1 Look at the following examples of horoscopes for three of the twelve signs:

AQUARIUS (January 20–February 18)
Long term plans and ambitions are accented and you can turn a positive mood, a sense of adventure, to your advantage. New ideas, as well as friendly contacts, spell success, but do not take unnecessary risks.

PISCES (February 19–March 20)
Cash and career matters should get a minor boost today; doubts and indecisions of the recent past could soon be swept away as fresh incentives appear. Prepare now for a busy, but rather fortunate, period soon about to begin and pare down routine activities.

ARIES (March 21–April 20)
Mars, your ruling star, is nicely aspected and makes this a promising day for partnerships. Any sort of co-operative activity will go with a swing, with companions willing to adapt to your ideas.

Use the above to help you write a horoscope for your partner for next week.

2 Write the ideal horoscope for yourself — one that you would love to read in a newspaper.

Unit 7   Doodling

A1   Doodles are those apparently meaningless drawings, patterns, scrawls and scribbles that are usually done in moments when you are, or ought to be, paying attention to something else. People often doodle when they are bored . . . in lectures or meetings for example . . . or when they are concentrating hard, thinking about what to say next in a letter, for example. Can you think of the moments when *you* doodle? Are these moments the same for you as for other members of the group? All of us doodle at some time or another and, according to popular psychology, there may be more to doodling than meets the eye. In fact, doodles may provide a key to your character as revealing as your zodiac sign!

To find out if this is so for you, try doing the activity below. Two sets of doodles are given (I and II) — but they are incomplete. Work with a partner. One of you should complete the first set of doodles (I) and the other should complete the second set (II). You should add something (*eg.* lines, shapes, etc.) to each of the six squares in the set.

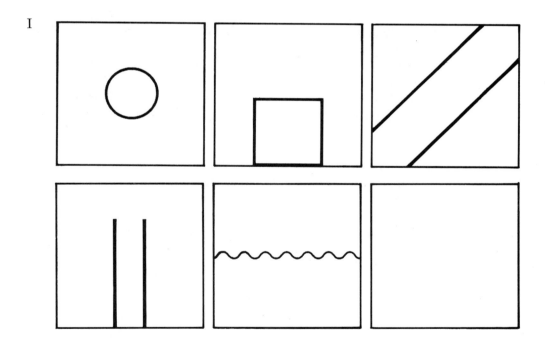

II

2 Exchange books so that you have in front of you your partner's completed doodles. Turn to the appropriate analysis on pages 169–172 and interpret the doodles done by your partner. (Make sure you don't look at the other analysis.) Make brief notes on your findings.

3 Now use the notes to tell your partner how you have analysed his/her character. Discuss the accuracy of each other's findings in relation to what you know about your own character.

B Writing

1 Use the notes you made earlier to write an analysis of your partner's character as revealed by the activity.

2 Copy the uncompleted doodles onto a piece of plain paper and ask a friend or relative to do the activity. Write a character analysis based on your findings.

Unit 8 Making New Friends

A Imagine you have been in London for a month. Although you have had some contact with people, you have found it difficult to make friends. You come across the following advertisement in a magazine:

It seems as if this might be the opportunity you have been looking for and you decide to go along to the introductory talk. At the talk you are given an application form to fill in and invited along to an informal get-together the following week to meet other new members.

Invent the personal details of an imaginary person and fill in the application form on the next page.

<u>Application Form</u>

Surname:

Other Names:

Age:

Nationality:

Profession/Job:

Interests	Tick (✓)	Give Details
Sport Reading Cinema Theatre Music Travel Food Going out Others		

B1 Now go along to the get-together. Try to talk to everybody and find out who the other people are, where they come from and, in particular, whether you have interests in common. Obviously you cannot make friends with everybody; so decide which of these people you would most like to see again.

2 Tell the class about the people you met at the get-together who you found particularly interesting.

C Writing

Either write a letter to someone you met at the get-together and want to meet again; invite him/her to meet you again and suggest arrangements (*eg.* what you are going to do, where and when, etc.).

Or Write a letter to a friend giving in as much detail as possible your first impressions of the person you most liked at the get-together.

You and Your Environment

9	Give Us Our Daily Drugs	*page* 36
10	Sharing a Home	39
11	Housing Ⓣ	43
12	Your Neighbourhood	45
13	Travel to Work	47
14	Teenagers' Leisure and Pleasure Ⓣ	51
15	How Much Do You Know about Whales?	54

Unit 9 Give Us Our Daily Drugs

In Britain caffeine, nicotine, alcohol and barbiturates are all legal drugs. They are similar to illegal ones in that, sooner or later, they can affect you so that you find yourself depending on a regular supply of them. The extent of dependence varies according to the person and the drug, but most people find it harder to give up even cigarettes or tea, than say, apples or cheese. This is because most of us smoke, have a coffee or drink either as a way of calming ourselves down and relieving tension or as a way of bucking ourselves up, finding extra energy. These drugs become associated with their power to relieve certain feelings and a habit is formed.

Stronger drugs — such as opiates and cocaine — can be habit-forming in just the same way. The drug taker comes to rely on the effect of the drug to produce a sensation of well-being and this reliance increases, until eventually dependence on a continual supply of the drug is established and an addictive habit is formed.

Ⓚ A1 Who Uses Drugs and Why?

People who are addicted to drugs can be of any age and walk of life. Their reasons for taking drugs are as varied as the environments in which they live. In some cases, addiction will be life-long; in others, it may be a temporary phase which can be broken out of.

In the left hand column there are notes on 5 cases of typical drug takers. Read them and try to match them with the most likely 'futures' from the column on the right; indicate your choices in the boxes below:

Drug Takers

1

Age 25. Painter and sculptor by inclination but has to do occasional labouring jobs to help make ends meet. Shares small studio flat with his girl-friend. 'Dropped out' of university after one year to go to art school. Has smoked pot irregularly ever since then for pleasure and for inspiration. Recently tried LSD and now takes it every few weeks believing it helps his work. Well aware of the dangers of heroin and thinks he would never try it.

2

Age 65. Bedridden at home ever since a serious operation two years ago. Afterwards in great pain and unable to sleep. Given barbiturates by doctor to help her sleep. Continued to demand barbiturates from doctor even when pain stopped because they were a great comfort and

Futures

A

Never too late to be honest with doctor about her dependence. Could probably be cured by treatment, maybe in mental hospital, but may later be tempted to use pills again. The longer she continues taking pills the more ill she will become and the harder a cure will be.

B

Almost sure to give up pills within a few years, but might find it impossible. If so, may become mentally disturbed or turn to 'hard' drugs.

put her in a dreamy state of well-being. Much preferred this to the boredom and anxieties of being bedridden. Now dependent on barbiturates.

3

Age 35. Housewife. Lives at home with husband and two kids. Always found housework, children and entertaining rather a strain. Rather fat after birth of second child. Doctor prescribed amphetamines for slimming: they also made her more cheerful and energetic. Soon needed more and more pills. Now dependent on them and has to trick chemist to get enough.

4

Age 19. Plays bass guitar with fairly successful group. Lives in communal pad with other group members. Time mostly spent in travelling in group van to and from one-night stands. Smoked pot regularly for last two years. Wrongly considers he needs it to play well. Recently started taking amphetamine pills to overcome fatigue of work. Also takes LSD occasionally for kicks. Has never taken heroin but friends have and some are addicts.

5

Age 16. At school, leaving soon. Lives at home. Out most evenings, sometimes on date, usually with friends. Most weekends at 'all-nighters', clubs or parties. First given a pill by a friend at a party. Started taking 'blues' most weekends because everyone else did and because it prevented tiredness. Soon started taking more for kicks. Had to take increasing numbers to repeat the same effect. Always very brought down on Mondays. Once tried pot but it had no effect.

C

Whilst in the pop-music world is unlikely to stop using drugs. Probably will stick to pot but could try 'hard' drugs and might become addicted. May become dependent on pot.

D

Because of her age and condition her doctor is unlikely to stop her supply of barbiturates. Most likely to continue taking them until her death.

E

Frustration of career could lead to 'hard' drugs but probably he will stick to 'soft' ones. May change his mind about them helping his work and give them up altogether, but this is unlikely unless he can cut himself off from his friends who are mostly 'hippy' drug-takers.

Drug takers:	1	2	3	4	5
Futures:					

2 Check and compare your answers with your partner.

Ⓚ **B Vocabulary**
1 Find words or phrases that have a similar meaning to the following:

    (i) earn enough money to survive *(case 1)*
    (ii) confined to bed due to illness *(case 2)*
    (iii) depressed *(case 5)*
    (iv) something which brings a person back to health *(future A)*
    (v) continue to use *(future C)*
    (vi) isolate from *(future E)*

2 Some of the language in the notes you have read is very colloquial. Can you work out what the following mean from the context in which they occur?

    (i) 'dropped out' *(case 1)*
    (ii) pad *(case 4)*
    (iii) one-night stands *(case 4)*
    (iv) for kicks *(cases 4 and 5)*

C Discuss these drug cases with the rest of the class. How many of them would be typical in your own country?

D1 Here are two more typical cases. Choose *one* and write what you think his future is likely to be.

(i) Age 55. Doctor, unmarried, lives alone above his surgery. For a long time has been unhappy about being greatly over-worked under lousy conditions. As a doctor has easy access to dangerous drugs. Two years ago, when depressed, took morphine. After that turned to morphine more and more often whenever things seemed too much. Now dependent on it.

His future:

(ii) Age 26. Professional racing cyclist. Lives at home with wife. At first did badly as professional. Decided to quit but friends persuaded him to try stimulants. First tried caffeine then amphetamines. Started winning races. Now always uses stimulants for racing.

His future:

2 Now exchange books with your partner and read each other's version. Discuss any differences.
3 Discuss your different opinions of the futures of the above two drug-takers with the rest of the class.

E Writing
Invent and describe a similar case of drug-taking and make predictions about the person's future.

Unit 10   Sharing a Home

When we think of our 'environment' we tend to think about many of the major problems facing mankind in the last quarter of the 20th century — energy, pollution, famine, conservation, etc. But our environment also includes our immediate surroundings — the place where we live.

Many people in Britain, especially in big cities, do not live with their families. This may be out of choice, for example, in the case of students learning English in London, or necessity, for example, people who have moved to major cities to find work. For whatever reason, it is often more pleasant and less lonely to share a flat or house with others than to live in digs or a hostel on your own.

A1   If you are looking for a room in a shared home or if you have one to offer, it is a good idea to put an advertisement in the small ad. columns of a local newspaper or magazine.

First of all, though, make sure you are familiar with the abbreviations used. The list below will help you:

o/r	own room	p.c.m.	per calendar month
s/c	self-contained	incl.	inclusive (of bills)
c.h.	central heating	excl.	exclusive (of bills)
p.w.	per week	refs.	references
p.m.	per month	m/f	male/female

2   The two extracts which follow are taken from the advertisement columns of London's magazine *Time Out*. Look through them and try to find suitable accommodation for the people advertising in the 'Flats Wanted' column by consulting the 'Flats/Rooms Offered' column. Write the appropriate letter in the boxes provided. If you find nothing suitable then leave the space blank.

Flats Wanted

1   ● MALE, 29, Leftish social worker/musician, non-smoker, semi-vegetarian, fair cook, brilliant baker, seeks o/r in mixed house, N1, N5, E. Anything.

☐

2   ● FEMALE seeks o/r in wholefoods vegetarian non-smoking household.

☐

Flats/Rooms Offered

A   ● PUTNEY, Second female, 27, non-smoker, share comfortable c.h. garden flat. Own room. Ideal person will be domesticated, sociable, independent, slightly highbrow and tolerant of decorating in progress. £16 p.w.

B   ● CONSIDERATE PERSON to share SW2 flat. Own room, use of garden. £58 monthly.

3 ● YOUNG LADY, 28, executive with very well behaved miniature Dachshund urgently seek accommodation London. Reasonable rent paid and/or willing cook/babysit occasionally. Refs.

☐

4 ● FRIENDLY and responsible female arts graduate (24) seeks own room north or central London

☐

5 ● PROFESSIONAL couple require furnished accommodation, preferably near Central London. Rent negotiable.

☐

6 ● FEMALE secretary seeks preferably quiet room under £15 in communal household.

☐

7 ● WANTED SOMEWHERE TO LIVE for 2 people (not a couple) in South West or Central London. No particularly disgusting habits.

☐

8 ● DAVID, 22, ARTIST seeks o/r in sociable flatshare. Any area considered £15 p.w. max.

☐

C ● KENSINGTON off park large double bedroom in very large groundfloor flat, suit friendly professional couple/singles to share with single guy 27. £173 p.c.m.

D ● VEGETARIAN GIRL, non-smoker, to share light, pleasant flat near Turnpike Lane Tube. Own room. C.H. £18 p.w.

E ● DOG LOVERS, 21–30, male or female, to share large Wanstead house with garden. (Central line). Double room £26 p.w. Single £15 p.w. Inclusive.

F ● HIGHBURY N5 Couple or two people willing to share double room in communal house. Rent £50 p.m. per person inclusive till end of July.

G ● MAIDA VALE room in flat with professional musician with two cats. £48 p.c.m. excl. bills. £60 deposit.

H ● FEMALE GRADUATE? Small room in large, comfy flat, Swiss Cottage. Share with owner who's often away. £20 p.w. exclusive.

I ● GIRL OWN ROOM phone, fridge, cooker, £10 per week plus 1 hrs work per day.

J ● SOCIALIST m/f wanted for room in large semi-collective house in Brixton. Age 23+ £14 p.w.

3 Now compare and discuss your choices with your partner and the rest of the group.

B Writing

Imagine that you are looking for accommodation in London. Write an advertisement similar to those in the 'Flats Wanted' column above. Be careful to give information both about yourself and the kind of accommodation you require.

C1 Role-play

Imagine that two members of your class already share a flat and have put the advertisement ringed below into *The Times*:

FLAT SHARING

W14—Prof. girl (non-smoker) 22–26 yrs. share room in luxury flat. £17 p.w.

PRIMROSE HILL—Holiday letting from July for 1–2 people. Room in luxury penthouse maisonette. Close to Tube, park and shops.

CENTRAL LONDON—Third person own room in sunny, modern flat. 23+, non-smoker. £93 p.c.m. incl. Avail. Sept. 1st.

W10—New flat, all amenities. Second person to share. July–Sept. Own room and bath. Garden and balcony. £25 p.w.

NURSE (24) Urgently seeks own room in central area up to £20 p.w.

WANDSWORTH COMMON— Large room in family house, 9 mins. Victoria. £18 p.w. incl.

BARNES—Share flat, own room. £65 p.c.m.

DULWICH—2nd girl, own room. £15 p.w. incl.

YOUNG MARRIED COUPLE, husband (27) Indian/Norwegian, wife (21) Danish/Norwegian will be attending school in London from 1st October till 29th October, would very much like accommodation (double bedroom) in London with breakfast (preferably).

The rest of the class are looking for accommodation in London, see the advertisement and decide to apply.

2 Preparation for Role-play

(a) Flatmates

Several people have answered your advertisement and you have decided to hold informal interviews in your flat to find the most suitable applicant. Before the interviews, you need to prepare the following:

(i) Invent a name, age and occupation for yourselves.

(ii) Decide the kind of person you would like to share your flat with, *eg.* quiet and self-contained or sociable and extrovert.

(iii) Be ready to answer questions about the way you organise the flat, *eg.* How do you share the cooking/cleaning, etc.? Do you put money into a

41

'kitty'? How do you divide the phone bill? etc.

(iv) Prepare questions that will help you find out as much as you can about the occupation, interests, and life style of each applicant. This will help you decide after the interview which is the most compatible.

(b) *Applicants*

You have spent the last month looking for accommodation in London and are beginning to despair of finding somewhere that suits you. The *Times* advertisement you have marked looks ideal and you decide to go along to the informal interview. Work with a partner to prepare the following, before *one* of you is interviewed.

(i) Invent your name, age, occupation, interests, hobbies, etc.

(ii) Decide what kind of personality you are, *eg.* shy, vivacious, etc. Later, when you go to the interview, make sure that this comes across.

(iii) Prepare questions that you want to ask at the interview, *eg.* do they shop and eat communally or separately? How do they divide the cooking, household chores, etc.? Do they object to loud music, coming in late, etc?

3 *Interviews*

The two flatmates should now interview all the applicants in front of the whole group.

If you are not being interviewed, listen carefully and note down words which describe the personality of each applicant. Be ready also to say which applicant you would choose.

4 *Follow-up*

(i) *Flatmates:* Discuss and decide which applicant you want to move into your flat.

Announce your decision to the group, explaining the reasons for your choice and justifying them, if necessary.

(ii) Now compare the different words noted during the interviews to describe the personality of each applicant. How far do they correspond with the personality each was trying to convey?

D Writing

1 As a result of the interview you have been offered a room in the shared flat. Write a letter accepting the offer.

2 A friend has recently moved to your home town but has not yet found accommodation. You have a spare room in your home. Write a letter inviting your friend to stay until he/she can find something more permanent.

Unit 11 Housing

A1 Look carefully at the pictures of different types of housing and match them with the descriptions below. Indicate your choice by writing the appropriate letter in the spaces provided.

(i)   row of two-storey brick-built terraced houses ☐

(ii) modern high-rise blocks of flats ☐

(iii) semi-detached houses with own gardens ☐

(iv) detached houses on a modern estate ☐

(v)   family house integrated into natural surroundings ☐

(vi) up-to-date family bungalow ☐

2 Look at the pictures again and answer the following questions about each:
   (a) Where would you expect to find this type of housing? *eg.* in the country, in the city centre, on the outskirts, in the suburbs, etc.
   (b) What kind of people would you expect to find living there? *eg.* rich, well-off, poor, etc.

3 Discuss your answers with your partner and see whether you agree.

4 Now work with your partner and make a list of the advantages and disadvantages of living in each type of housing, *eg.* far from the shops, difficult to get to know your neighbours, etc.

5 Compare and discuss the advantages and disadvantages you have found in each area with the rest of the group.

6 Which type of housing would *you* like to live in most? Which type of housing would *you* like to live in least? Discuss and explain the reasons for your choices.

Ⓣ Ⓚ **B1** You are now going to listen to a tape in which 3 speakers talk about their ideal type of housing. Listen to the tape and fill in the table below:

	Present Type of Housing	Main Problems of Present Housing	Ideal Type of Housing	Main Features of Ideal Housing
Speaker I				
Speaker II				
Speaker III				

Ⓣ **2** Compare and check your answers with your partner. Listen to the tape again if necessary.

C1 Look at the table and decide which type of ideal housing you prefer. Discuss your opinions with your partner.

2 Discuss your own ideas for an ideal type of housing with the rest of the class. How similar are your ideas?

D Writing

1 Write a description of the type of housing that you think would be ideal. Explain the reasons for your choice.

2 Imagine that there is a proposal to create a badly-needed new residential area on the outskirts of your town. At the moment it is planned to build twelve new blocks of flats like those in Picture *f* as this is the cheapest and quickest way of providing housing for lots of people. Write a letter to the Town Council *either* in support of the proposal *or* criticising it and putting forward an alternative plan. In either case give reasons to justify your opinion.

Unit 12   Your Neighbourhood

A1   For most people, it is not only the type of housing which is important, but the whole neighbourhood or community which we live in as well. Sociologists agree that it is essential to keep urban residential areas on a human scale — in other words, to keep them of a size where they are felt to be social units by the inhabitants and where people can share the variety of communal services and amenities that are available.

Look at the list below and decide which *10* amenities you consider most important to have in your neighbourhood, *ie.* within walking distance of your home. Indicate your choices by writing a cross (×) next to each item in the list you choose.

1 Cinema	16 Police station
2 Railway station	17 Off-licence
3 Market	18 Creche
4 Swimming baths	19 Nursery school
5 Park or garden	20 Primary school
6 Café	21 Secondary school
7 Pub	22 Launderette
8 Restaurant	23 Church
9 Bank	24 Theatre
10 Post Office	25 Concert hall
11 Hospital	26 Small shops (for everyday things)
12 Library	27 Supermarket
13 Doctor's surgery	28 Shopping centre (with variety
14 Dental surgery	of shops, *eg.* clothes and
15 Community centre (for	furniture)
meetings, dances,	29 Old people's home
amateur theatricals,	30 Sportsfields (for football,
etc.)	hockey, etc.)

2   Compare and discuss your choices with your partner. Explain your reasons for choosing each item and, if you don't agree, try to bring your partner round to sharing your point of view.

You *must come to an agreement* over what the 10 most important amenities are before moving on to the next activity.

B1   Now look at the map of an imaginary neighbourhood on p. 46. At the moment only the street names and residential areas are marked — the rest is up to you! Work with your partner and add to the map the ten essential amenities you have chosen in the locations that you think would most benefit the whole community. Indicate your arrangement by writing the number of the items you choose in the appropriate place on the map. Then add them to the key below the map in the space provided.

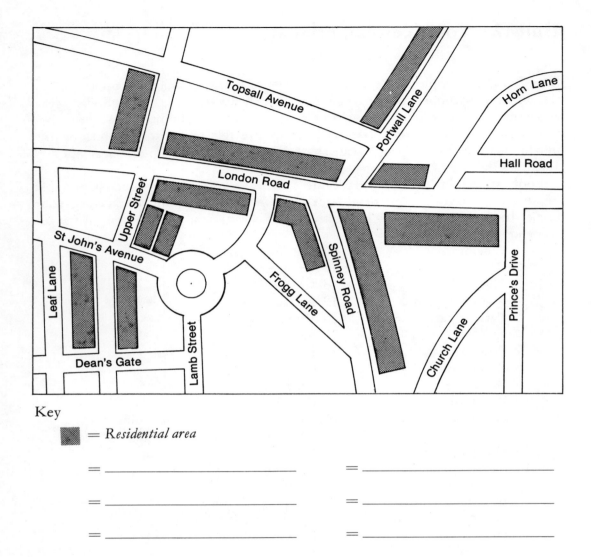

Key

■ = *Residential area*

= _____   = _____

= _____   = _____

= _____   = _____

= _____   = _____

= _____   = _____

C Now work with your partner and another pair and discuss and criticise each other's choice of essential amenities and the way you have arranged them on the map.

D Discuss your ideas with the whole group. How far do you all agree? Which plan do you think is best?

E Writing
1 Use the completed map to write a description of the neighbourhood you have planned.
2 The Town Council is planning to redevelop your neighbourhood. Write a letter outlining the improvements you would like to see.

Unit 13   Travel to Work

Ⓚ **A1**   People who travel a reasonable distance to work by public or private transport are known as *commuters*. The article you are going to read outlines recent trends in commuting in Britain.

Read the article on p. 48 and find out the following:

1 The general trend in commuting

  a by car: _____   *b* by bus: _____

2 The trend as regards commuting into central London:

_____

3 The trend as regards commuting elsewhere in Britain:

_____

4 The proportion of workers living within 10 miles of their place of work:

_____

5 *(i)* The percentage of users of cars, vans or lorries

  in

1965	1972/73	1975/76

 (ii) The average number of passengers in each car

  in

1965	1972/73	1975/76

6 The effect on commuting of the 1973 Israeli/Arab war:

_____

7 The means of travel to and from work in relation to people's age and sex. Complete the table below:

Means of Travel	Main Users: Male/Female	Age Range	% of Users in Age Range
1 Public Transport (especially bus)			
2a Car/Van/Lorry			
2b Car/Van/Lorry			
3 Bicycles			
4 On Foot*			

* 'On Foot'＝people who walk over a mile to and from their place of work.

Broadly speaking, commuting by car has grown since the second world war, and fewer people have travelled to work by public transport — particularly by bus. The south-east of England has perhaps become more like the rest of the country. While commuting into central London has dropped, as it has to other city centres that have lost jobs, people in the rest of the country have become more willing to travel further to their employment.

Even so, over four-fifths of the country's workforce still lives within ten miles of its job. Between 1965 and 1975–76 the average journey to work lengthened from 4.8 miles to 5.8 miles.

Although the most recent National Travel Survey data relates to 1975–76, and therefore probably understates the increased use of motorcycles and mopeds suggested by sale and registration figures, the overwhelming trend in recent decades has been the growing use of motor cars for getting to work. The NTS groups together cars, vans and lorries. Whereas they accounted for only 35 per cent of journeys to work in 1965, they were up to 54 per cent by 1972–73.

Nor did the energy alarms of the early seventies put a rapid brake on this dependence. By 1975–76 these vehicles were responsible for 59 per cent of journeys to work. Car sharing did not increase as a result either: mean car occupancy on such journeys, which fell from 1.32 to 1.27 between 1965 and 1972–73, stayed at the same level over the following three years. In fact, the only small adjustments which took place in the aftermath of the Yom Kippur war (1973) were tiny rises in bicycling and walking to work. Both rose by 1 per cent.

There are sharp contrasts between modes of travel to work according to sex and earning power. The keenest users of public transport, especially the buses, are women aged 16 to 20: 51 per cent of them get to work in this way. Similarly, it's middle-aged men — aged between 30 and 59 — who are most likely to drive to work: 64 per cent travel to work by car, van or lorry, only 3 per cent more than their younger successors, aged 21 to 29.

Among self-propelled means of transport, the highest rating for bicyclists is among men aged 60 to 64 — (10 per cent of their journeys to work). Women aged 60 to 64 are most likely to walk to work (37 per cent). As Mayer Hillman, of the Policy Studies Institute, has pointed out, the official statistics find it difficult to cope with walking; although it is an ingredient in all door-to-door journeys to work, it is sometimes excluded where it amounts to less than a mile.

2   Check your answers with your partner and see whether you agree. Do you find any of the above statistics surprising?

B1   *Survey:* How do the members of your class come to their English lessons?

Get up out of your seat and carry out interviews with a maximum of *10* fellow students about the means of transport they use to come to school. Ask also about the distance between home and school, the time the journey usually takes, the cost and any particular problems connected with the journey. Write the information you receive in the table on the next page.

Name of Student	Means of Transport	Distance Travelled	Time Journey Takes	Cost per Day	Problems Connected with Journey
1					
2					
3					
4					
5					
6					
7					
8					
9					
10					

2 Discuss your findings with the whole class. Are there any generalisations you can make about the way students in your class come to English lessons?

3 Writing
Now write a report on your findings in the class survey on 'travelling to school'. Try to give both specific examples supported by statistics and also general trends, if possible.

C1 Role-play
The council in your town has recently decided to ban all cars, vans and lorries from the town centre which they intend to turn into a large pollution-free pedestrian precinct. Plans include the building of huge car parks on the edges of the town from which buses (and taxis) will be available to take people into the centre. Cyclists will be allowed to ride their bicycles along special 'bike lanes' into the town centre. It is also planned to plant a large number of trees, bushes and plants to make the town centre a more attractive place. Public meetings to discuss these proposed changes will be organised.

A meeting is to be held in your area and below are some of the people who will attend it and the opinions they have about this controversial topic. Work in groups of 4–6 and assign one of the roles to each member of the group. If possible, there should be an equal number of people for and against the council's plans.

2 Preparation for Role-play

Assign one of the following roles to each member of the group:

A wealthy commuter — has driven a car to work for the last 10 years. Parks in firm's private car park. Outraged at inconvenience of having to park outside the town and take a bus.

Town resident — ardent conservationist, lives in town centre and feels enthusiastic about council's plans. Sees an end to pollution and noise — welcomes more trees, plants, etc.

Office employee — lives outside town but doesn't own a car. Welcomes the council's plans, hopes for improved and cheaper public transport.

A High Street supermarket manager — used to customers buying in bulk and loading goods into car. Very worried about severe loss of trade.

Taxi driver — very much in favour of plans. Sees great possibility for more work and more money!

Parent with three young children — lives outside the town. With small children finds it extremely difficult to shop in town without a car. Therefore, does not approve of plans.

Spend a few minutes individually thinking of further arguments to support the opinion you have been assigned.

3 Now hold the public meeting and discuss the issue with the other members of the group using the arguments you have prepared. Do your best to support those who have a similar point of view and to try and persuade those who don't agree with you that your point of view is right.

D Writing

Write an article for the local newspaper in which you summarise — as fairly as you can — the arguments discussed for and against the Council's plans as at the Public Meeting. Invent a suitable headline for your article.

Unit 14   Teenagers' Leisure and Pleasure

Ⓚ **A1**   Look at the following and write your answers in the spaces marked 'You'. (NB. For the moment do not write anything in the spaces marked 'Tape'.)
(i)   Put the following leisure activities in the order of popularity you think they have with sixteen-year olds. Write 1, 2 and 3 in the boxes.

	You	Tape
Playing Outdoor Games and Sports		
Reading Books (not school books)		
Watching TV		

(ii)   Which of the following do you think 16-year-old girls spend more money on? Indicate your choice by writing *a*, *b*, *c* or *d* in the box marked 'You'.

a Entertainment
b Clothes and cosmetics
c Cigarettes and drinks
d Records, tapes and books

You	Tape

(iii)   Which of the following do you think 16-year-old boys spend more money on? Indicate your choice by writing *a*, *b*, *c*, or *d* in the box marked 'You'.

a Entertainment
b Clothes
c Cigarettes and drinks
d Records, tapes and books

You	Tape

(iv)   The age of 16 is often considered to be a 'difficult' age. Which *three* adjectives from the list below do you think would best describe the behaviour of average 16-year-olds at home?

Write 1, 2 and 3 in the boxes marked 'You' to indicate your first, second and third choices.

	You	Tape			You	Tape
Fussy				Restless		
Bullying				Disobedient		
Lazy				Irritable		
Solitary				Bored		

2 Now discuss and compare your opinion with your partner.

Ⓣ **B1** Listen to the tape and answer the questions in A, in the spaces marked 'Tape', according to the interview. Compare your answers with the facts in the interview.

Ⓚ **2** Listen to the tape a second time and answer the following questions:

(i) How many teenagers took part in the survey? _____

(ii) When was the survey published? _____

(iii) Write in the boxes the percentages of 16-year-olds who often take part in the following activities:

	%
Playing Outdoor Games and Sports	
Reading Books (not school books)	
Watching TV	
Going to Parties	
Dancing at Discos	
Playing Indoor Games and Sports	

(iv) In the past what was often the visible difference between middle-class and working-class teenagers?

_____

_____

(v) Explain the common difference nowadays:

_____

_____

(vi) What possible explanation is given for parents not describing their own 16-year-old children's behaviour in the home as 'aggressive'?

_____

_____

3 Compare your answers first with your partner and then with the whole class.

4 Discuss your opinions about the ways teenagers spend their leisure time with the rest of the class. Do you think a similar survey carried out in your own country would produce similar results?

C1 Role-play

Imagine you are responsible for setting up a Youth Club in your area. You have been allocated a relatively small amount of money by the Town Council to help keep teenagers off the streets and to reduce juvenile delinquency and vandalism which have been on the increase. The Youth Club will be open four evenings a week from 7.30 pm–11 pm.

Work in groups of three or four and plan the kind of activities you think would be most likely to attract teenagers to your Club. You may wish to refer to the table below to guide you in your choices.

Leisure activities of 16-year-olds expressed as a percentage

	Often	Sometimes	Never or hardly ever	Like to but no chance
Reading books (apart from school work or homework)	27	46	24	3
Playing outdoor games and sports	38	35	24	3
Swimming	21	44	27	8
Playing indoor games and sports	25	32	32	10
Watching television	65	29	5	1
Going to parties in friends' homes	19	48	26	7
Dancing at dance halls, discos etc.	39	31	24	5
Voluntary work to help others	7	30	46	16

Decide in your groups on the *four* activities you consider will be most successful and work out details of setting them up.

2 Now discuss your proposed activities with the other groups and decide which four activities are best overall to concentrate on.

D Writing

Write a report to the Town Council outlining your proposals for the Youth Club you have discussed. Explain and justify your choice of activities.

Unit 15 How Much Do You Know about Whales?

A1 Below and on the next two pages you will find an article on whales. Before reading it work with a partner and try to answer the questions below — if you don't know have a guess!

DO NOT READ THE ARTICLE YET!

    (i) What sort of creatures are whales? (Fish? Reptiles? Mammals?)

    _____

   (ii) Where do they live? (Sea? Rivers? Lakes?)

    _____

  (iii) What other creatures belong to the same family?

    _____

  (iv) What is the greatest length a whale can grow to?

    _____

   (v) What is the maximum weight of an adult whale?

    _____

  (vi) What do they normally eat? _____

 (vii) How fast can they swim? _____

(viii) Do they have a sense of   smell? _____

                                sight? _____

                              hearing? _____

                                taste? _____

  (ix) What commercial products are made from whales?

    _____

   (x) What danger is there of whales becoming extinct?

    _____

2 How far do your answers/impressions correspond with those of the other students?

B1 NOW READ THE ARTICLE BELOW TO SEE HOW RIGHT YOU WERE.

WHALES

The term whale is often employed by scientists as a general name for the larger members of the order Cetacea, a group of primarily marine mammals (and therefore warm-blooded and breathing through the lungs) occurring throughout the seas of the world and in certain tropical rivers and lakes. Most of the smaller members of the order are called dolphins or porpoises. Their ancestors were land-living creatures that started to colonise the sea and some fresh-water systems some 100 million years ago. They bear a superficial resemblance to fish, and indeed were originally classified as such many years ago.

54

A General Features:

(i) Size and Weight:

The order Cetacea includes two distinct living suborders: Odontoceti, the modern toothed whales; and Mysticeti, the baleen whales which lack teeth. The odontocetes include about 70 species including the porpoises, dolphins, killer whales and spermwhales. They range in length from about 1.3 metres (4.3 feet) in the smaller porpoises to about 18 metres (60 feet) in the male sperm whale. The length of the 10 species of baleen whales ranges from 6 metres (20 feet) to about 30 metres (just under 100 feet) in the largest recorded specimen of the blue whale. A great range of adult weight is encompassed by the Cetacea, from about 45 kilograms (100 lbs) in some small porpoises to about 136,000 kilograms (150 tons) in the blue whale.

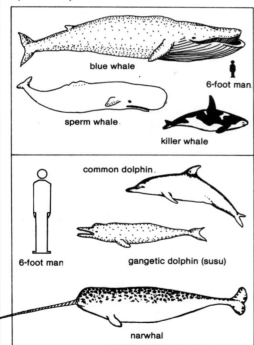

(ii) Breathing:

Breathing is accomplished at the water surface through their blow-holes which are generally located on top of the head. The exhalation produces the familiar spout. Following inhalation, the animal holds its breath for variable periods, as it swims below the surface. Dives of smaller cetaceans last a few minutes but those of some larger species may last an hour and perhaps longer.

(iii) Behaviour:

Most toothed whales spend their entire lives in tightly organised schools which may range in numbers from a few animals to 1,000 or more individuals. Baleen whales are more often found singly, although small schools occur on the breeding grounds, and whales may congregate in feeding areas in considerable numbers. Schools of toothed whales may be quite complex in structure, involving family groups, groups segregated by age and sex, and even schools composed of two or more species. Groups of mothers with young are usually found together near the centre of a school.

(iv) Feeding:

Two general modes of feeding exist in cetaceans. Baleen whales are strainers, ie. they sieve planktonic organisms from the water. Toothed whales, on the other hand, actively pursue and capture swimming prey, especially fish and squid.

(v) Speed:

It has been reported that porpoises travel at speeds of at least 38 kilometres per hour (24 mph) and whales at 56 kph (35 mph).

(vi) Migration:

Most baleen whales undergo seasonal migrations, some as long as 3,000 miles (5,000 kms) each way from feeding to breeding grounds. With the exception of the sperm whale the migrations of toothed whales seem to be much more local in character and in some species apparently do not occur at all.

(vii) Communication:

Acoustic behaviour, which is highly developed in all cetaceans, involves passive listening, social signalling and echolocation, ie. using the echoes of their own signals for navigation. Low-pitched sounds, such as barks, whistles, screams and moans, seem to serve mostly in social communication whereas brief clicks of high-intensity sound serve largely in navigation. Captive porpoises have mimicked human voice signals and artificial sounds and a variety of sounds have been shaped by training techniques. No evidence exists, however, for a humanoid language in any cetacean.

(viii) The Senses:
Smell: The sense of smell is reduced or lacking in cetaceans.
Sight: Underwater vision has been tested only in porpoises; it is excellent except in the case of some river porpoises.
Hearing: Hearing is a major sense in all cetaceans. In the bottle-nosed dolphin, for example, hearing capability extends through the human range to about ten times the human upper limit.
Taste: Marked food preferences have been noted in captive odontocetes. The presence of well-developed taste buds on the tongue point to a well developed sense of taste.

B   Importance to Man:

Many of the more abundant whales and porposies are commercially important, their meat being used as food for animals and (especially in Japan) for humans and their oil for industrial lubrication and for conversion into soaps and fatty acids, which are used in cosmetics and detergents.

C   Whaling

(i) About two dozen countries have engaged in commercial whaling at one time or other, but by the early 1970s only Japan and the Soviet Union maintained whaling fleets in open ocean, the fleets of other countries having ceased operations as a result of declining markets for whale products and drastically reduced populations of the commercially valuable whales. Several other countries have continued to take whales from shore stations; eg. in the Azores, where whaling is still practised largely in the same manner as it was during the nineteenth century. Limitations on catches of the larger cetaceans, imposed by the International Whaling Commission (IWC), were too late to prevent the near extinction through overexploitation of the blue whale by the late 1950s. Populations of the fin whale have declined sharply under heavy fishing pressure. The decline in these species has led to increased pressure on the sei whale and the sperm whale. Whales swimming in international waters used to be regarded as a common and free resource. The only costs to the whalers are their boats, fuel, processing equipment and labour. The commercial returns can be formidable: at least £100,000 for a single blue whale.

(ii) The modern method of killing a whale is by means of a grenade-tipped harpoon, weighing 160 lbs, which is fired at 60 mph into the whale's flesh and which explodes inside the body. Several harpoons may be fired into a single animal. A nylon line runs from the harpoon to a controlling power winch, which is used to bring in the whale when it has become exhausted. In spite of this weaponry, large whales sometimes tow catcher-boats many miles.

(Adapted from the articles on *Whales* and *Whaling* in *Encyclopaedia Britanica* and from a handout on *Whales* produced by Friends of the Earth Ltd.)

2 Who knew the most about whales? Are you surprised by any of the facts you have read? If so, which? Discuss your opinions with the rest of the class.

3 Now read section **A** on General Features again and fill in the table below:

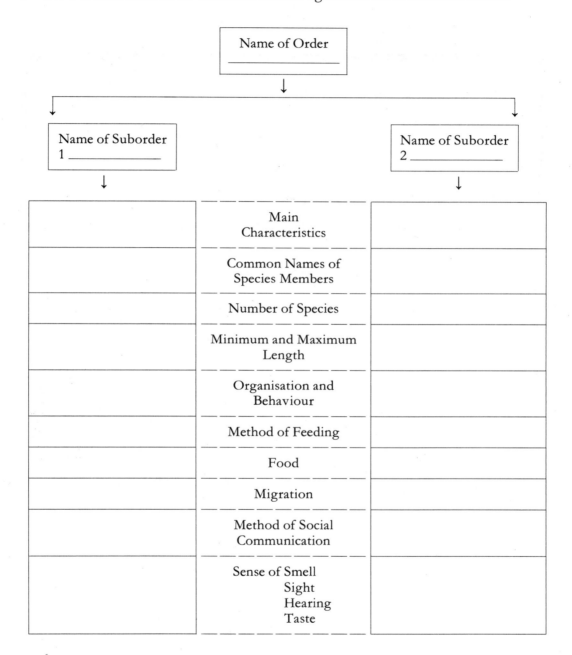

4 Check and compare your answers first with your partner and then with the rest of the class.

C As a result of information such as that below, you and some friends have decided to organise a two-day campaign, which will take place over a week-end in the near future, to help save whales from extinction. Your aims are to make the public more aware of the whale's plight and to raise funds to cover this publicity.

In groups of 4–6 work out what you plan to do.

Friends of the Earth give the following estimates to show the drastic decline in the number of whales:

	Estimated Original Population	Estimated Current Population	Percentage of Original Population
Blue Whale	195,000	6,000	3%
Bowhead Whale	50,000	3,000	6%
Humpback Whale	105,000	6,000	5%
Right Whale	120,000	4,000	3%

D Writing

1 Write a letter to your local newspaper outlining your campaign proposals and asking for public support.

2 In a similar way to the article on whales, and using the same or similar headings, write an article on any other animal that you feel is in danger of becoming extinct. Look at encyclopaedias and other reference books for information and ideas.

You and the Media

16	What the Papers Said	*page*	60
17	A Foreign Correspondent Ⓣ		66
18	The Soap Opera		69
19	Children and Television Ⓣ		71
20	The Language of Advertising		75
21	Consumer Discrimination		78
22	A Change Is as Good as a Rest Ⓣ		81

Unit 16   What the Papers Said

Ⓚ   A1   Read the following article from *The Times* and complete the table below. Put a cross ($\times$) in a column if no information is mentioned in the article.

From Arthur Osman
Birmingham

After the publication yesterday of the Government's report on the smallpox outbreak at Birmingham University two years ago the only fact that appeared to be undisputed was that it would never be known how Mrs Janet Parker, aged 40, caught the infection from which she died.

Mrs Parker was a photographer who worked in a department above the laboratory in the medical school where the virus was kept.

Publication of the report was delayed for amendments to be made by Mr Patrick Jenkin, Secretary of State for Social Services, to his foreword. That came after vigorous criticism of the report and its proposed publication by the university, which also went to Mrs Margaret Thatcher.

Mr Jenkin said in the amended foreword that it was not for him to enter into controversy on evidence which might be conflicting.

Professor Henry Bedson, aged 48, virologist, who was head of the laboratory, killed himself after Mrs Parker became infected.

The university was prosecuted before Birmingham justices last November by the Health and Safety Executive on the substance of yesterday's delayed report. The case was dismissed after a fortnight's hearing after the university stated that the report was substantially incorrect.

Mr Jenkin said yesterday that despite last year's prosecution it did not detract from the report's public importance. "The report had clearly to be read in the knowledge of the circumstances in which it was prepared, of the conclusion of the justices and of the persisting uncertainty about the way in which the outbreak occurred.

"However, that does not detract from the public importance and value of the general recommendation it contains about the inspection of laboratories where work with very dangerous pathogens is carried out, and about procedures for notification and control.

"I believe it important that these recommendations should be widely known. On some of them action has already been taken and on others consultations initiated by the Health and Agriculture Departments and the Health and Safety Executive are in progress."

The original typewritten script of the report, by Professor Reginald Shooter and his colleagues, was "leaked" to the press in January, 1979, by Mr Clive Jenkins, general secretary of the Association of Scientific, Technical and Managerial Staffs. The union is handling a civil claim for damages by Mrs Parker's widower. Professor Shooter is Dean of the Medical College at St Bartholomew's Hospital, London.

Birmingham University had alleged that 19 errors had been made by the Shooter committee, of which 10 were totally untrue. Others were described as "red herrings" or being "completely discredited" by evidence given to the court last year. They also use the words tendentious, irrelevant or speculative about other parts.

The report found that because of poor laboratory procedures opportunities existed for virus particles to become airborne and to be transferred to surfaces. The result was that the animal pox room could become heavily contaminated. "This represented a major breach in containment policy."

It was suggested that the most probable way Mrs Parker was infected was through a duct in the outer animal pox room to the telephone room immediately above. When seated at the telephone she used several times a day she would have been close to an ill-fitting inspection panel of the duct.

The transfer of virus had probably occurred in one of three ways: on an air current, by personal contact, or by contact with contaminated equipment or apparatus leaving the laboratory. "We believe that the airborne route through the duct to the telephone room is the most probable way by which Mrs Parker was infected because this seems to be the one route that could have selectively affected her."

The university denied that in a statement saying that based on the evidence to the court the cabinet was perfectly satisfactory, and another in the animal pox laboratory was never used for smallpox work.

Tests had shown the possible spread of particles in the building was based on four false propositions, which made them worthless as evidence.

There is no evidence that Mrs Parker ever used this telephone on any relevant occasions.

Name	Job	Employer	Age	Main Part in the Story
1 Janet Parker				
2 Patrick Jenkin				
3 Henry Bedson				
4 Clive Jenkins				
5 Reginald Shooter				

2 Check your answers with your partner. If you differ look again at the article together.

Ⓚ 3 Read the passage again and answer the following:
- (i) Why was publication of the report delayed?
- (ii) What was the outcome of the court case against the University?
- (iii) Why did the Government spokesman, Mr Jenkin, say he wanted the report widely read?
- (iv) What was the University's reaction to the report?
- (v) What was the main criticism made of the University laboratory?
- (vi) How was it most likely that Janet Parker caught smallpox?

4 Check your answers with your partner. If you differ look again at the article together.

B Here are two other articles on the same topic published on the same day in *(i) The Sun* and *(ii)* the *Daily Mail*.

(i) The Sun 25/7/80

by Leo Clancy

THE FULL horror of how blundering incompetence nearly caused a smallpox epidemic was officially revealed in a grim report yesterday.

It tells how warnings were ignored and safety regulations flouted at a Birmingham University laboratory experimenting with killer viruses.

A woman medical photographer at the university caught smallpox and died in 1978.

The professor in charge of the laboratory, Henry Bedson, later killed himself by slashing his throat.

The report kept secret by the Government for 18 months, reveals that only prompt action—and chance—prevented a major smallpox epidemic.

The document, drawn up by an inquiry team led by top professor Reginald Shooter...

● **CLAIMS** that Professor Bedson made misleading reports about safety standards in the lab.

● **ACCUSES** the university of not training staff properly, and

● **SLAMS** the Department of Health and other authorities for failing in safety duties.

The inquiry team did not discover exactly how the deadly virus reached photographer Janet Parker, 40.

But they claim that anyone working in the immediate vicinity of the lab could have caught smallpox.

Bench

Safety standards were so bad that some work was carried out on an open bench instead of inside a safety cabinet, says the report.

Legal action was taken, but the university was cleared of blame.

The report was leaked by union boss Clive Jenkins.

(ii) Daily Mail 25/7/80

by William Langley

POOR safety standards and inadequate staff training caused the fatal Birmingham smallpox outbreak, says a report published yesterday.

Research worker Mrs Janet Parker died and her mother was seriously infected when a virus escaped inside Birmingham University's Medical School in 1978.

A 215-page report by a team under Professor Reginald Shooter, of St Bartholomew's Hospital, London, says the outbreak could have been prevented. It accuses the university authorities of:

... Allowing inadequate sealing of ducts and inlets;

Insufficient sterilisation and disinfection;

Use of dangerous viruses outside safety cabinets.

The report says that Mrs Parker, a 40-year-old photographer for the unit, probably contracted the disease through a faulty air duct.

'Because of the poor laboratory procedures, the failure to use the safety cabinet for all open work with smallpox, the failure to use sealed containers to transport infected materials and the practice of passing in and out of the smallpox room during work without changing gowns or gloves or washing hands, we believe that opportunities existed for the virus particles to become airborne and to become transferred both in this way and by direct contact to surfaces.'

Of the only remaining smallpox research centre in Britain—St Mary's Medical School, Paddington—the report says: 'We think it no longer makes sense to have the country's remaining smallpox laboratory in a densely populated part of London.'

The Birmingham outbreak cost not only the life of Mrs Parker but that of research head Professor Henry Bedson, who cut his throat in the aftermath.

The Government decided to publish the report despite strong objections by the university for its suppression.

Professor Shooter's conclusions were the basis of an unsuccessful prosecution for negligence brought against the university authorities in November 1979.

The Department of Health yesterday declined to blame or absolve the university. Social Services Secretary Patrick Jenkin says in a foreword to the Shooter report: 'It is not for me to enter into controversy about matters on which the evidence may be in conflict.'

He said the report should be read in the knowledge that the university was cleared last November.

In an angry statement yesterday, the university said: 'It is a blemished report.'

'What has happened to British justice when the Government and its agencies, having failed in the courts, now invite a retrial by innuendo through a discredited document?'

Ⓚ **1** In the left-hand column below are the phrases used in *The Times* article to describe the report and the reaction to its publication (but *not* its detailed contents). Read the articles from *The Sun* and the *Daily Mail* and make a list of similar phrases in the columns below:

The Times	The Sun	Daily Mail
was delayed for amendments		
vigorous criticism . . . by the university		
public importance . . . and value of the general recommendation		
original typewritten script . . . was 'leaked' to the press		

Ⓚ **2** Check your lists with your partner. If you differ look again at the articles together.

Ⓚ **C1** Each newspaper uses rather different styles of language, *eg*. *The Times* said Professor Bedson 'killed himself', the *Daily Mail* said he 'cut his throat' and *The Sun* said he 'killed himself by slashing his throat'.

Working in pairs make a list of the words and phrases used in each of the three articles *to criticise the university*. The first one has been given in each case.

The Times	The Sun	Daily Mail
poor laboratory procedures	blundering incompetence	poor safety standards

2 Working in pairs decide how you would characterise the language of each article, *eg.* formal, dramatic, slangy, etc. What does it suggest about each newspaper?

D Here are the three headlines accompanying the articles. Match the headlines with the articles. Write S *(The Sun)*, T *(The Times)* and M *(Daily Mail)* in the boxes:

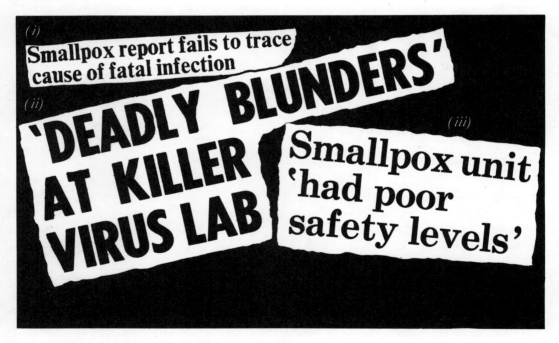

(i)	(ii)	(iii)

E Decide with your partner which you think is the best of the three articles. Discuss your opinion with the rest of the class.

Ⓚ **F Writing**

Here are two articles on the same topic — from *The Sun* and the *Daily Mail*. In small groups discuss how you think the same topic would be written up in *The Times*. Discuss your opinions with other groups and then rewrite these articles in the style you imagine to be appropriate to *The Times*. (The original *Times* article can be found on p. 178 of the Answer Key. Read this article only *after* you have completed the writing task.)

The Sun 25/7/80

JANET WINS BATTLE OF THE BRA

PRETTY Janet Lindley won a court-room tussle over her bra yesterday.

Two High Court judges cleared Janet of assaulting a policewoman who tried to strip her.

They ruled that magistrates boobed when they fined her £50.

Student Janet's bust-up with the law started when she was arrested for being drunk in a street two years ago.

She was taken to Exeter police station where WPC Irene Fry tried to remove her bra "in case she tried to hang herself."

Janet, 29, of Clifton Hill, Exeter, scratched and kicked the officer in the struggle, it was alleged.

After yesterday's hearing, Janet said: "Thank God it's all over.

"I felt very strongly about the police attempt to remove my bra. There were policemen present. You just don't humiliate people like that.

"When I was arrested, I had been celebrating my birthday."

"I think it was petty to bring an assault charge over an incident like this."

Lord Justice Donaldson and Mr Justice Mustill said they will give full judgment later, setting out guidelines on police rights.

Police claimed the case was an important test of their right to search prisoners.

Daily Mail 25/7/80

VICTORY FOR BRA GIRL

THE student fined £50 for assaulting a policewoman who tried to remove her bra won her appeal yesterday.

Two High Court judges upheld 29-year-old Janet Lindley's claim that magistrates should not have found her guilty.

The appeal was regarded by police as a test case on their right to search prisoners.

Lord Justice Donaldson and Mr Justice Mustill said that they would quash the conviction and give a full judgment later setting out guidelines on police rights.

Miss Lindley, of Clifton Hill, Exeter, who was originally arrested for being drunk and disorderly, was alleged to have scratched and kicked the police-woman.

Unit 17   A Foreign Correspondent

A   A foreign correspondent is a newspaper, radio or television reporter who is based abroad and sends back news to his employer. Briefly discuss what you think it is like to work as a foreign correspondent. What do you think are the advantages of such a job? What problems do you think there might be?

Ⓣ Ⓚ **B1**   Now listen to an interview with a foreign correspondent based in Lisbon, Portugal and answer the following questions:

1   The journalist works for _____ news agency.

2   How many large world agencies are there? _____

3   How long has he worked for this agency? _____

4   He has worked in _____ countries but has been based in:

    (i) _____

    (ii) _____

    (iii) _____

    (iv) _____

and is leaving Portugal for _____.

5   *Traditionally*, to enter journalism the following steps were taken:

6   Did he follow this pattern? _____

7   *Nowadays*:

8   Where can someone do an undergraduate degree in journalism? _____

9   In England which type of subject is it perhaps best to have studied at University? _____

10   What did *he* study at University? _____

11   How can one do an extra course (*ie*. after finishing university)?

    (i) _____

    (ii) _____

12 Who does he say journalists represent? _____

_____

13 Annually how many graduates apply to join this news agency? _____
How many are successful? _____
14 What determines what a journalist writes about? _____

_____

_____

15 Which part of the world does the agency mainly write for? _____
Why? _____

_____

16 Who owns this agency? _____
17 Where is it based? _____
18 How important does he consider the markets outside Europe? _____

_____

19 What other services are mentioned? _____

_____

20 What restrictions does a journalist have placed on him? _____

_____

21 In what circumstances can he not interview someone? _____

_____

22 What would he do if he realised a given story is likely to stir up
problems? _____
23 Who are the 'subscribers'? _____
24 Why do they want the agency man always to be there? _____

_____

🕭 **2** Now check your answers with your partner. If you differ listen again to the
interview together.

🕭 **C** Listen to the tape once more. Explain the meaning of the following words and
phrases in the context in which they are used:
> *(i)* I've worked off and on
> *(ii)* I had a rather mixed career
> *(iii)* the particular disciplines required
> *(iv)* representing the fourth estate
> *(v)* we have guidelines
> *(vi)* laws of libel
> *(vii)* the ruling on this sort of story
> *(viii)* to jeopardise the Reuter man
> *(ix)* get them in bad odour with the government
> *(x)* to be there through thick and thin

D Using the information you now have from the questions and answers above,
work in pairs and reconstruct the interview in your own words. One person should
play the part of the interviewer and ask the questions and the other should pretend
to be the foreign correspondent.

67

E Writing

Based on the information in the interview write a paragraph on one or more of the following:

(*i*) How to become a journalist.

(*ii*) The Reuter News Agency.

(*iii*) The journalist in the interview.

F Role-play

1 You are an imaginary famous person — a politician, a sportsman, a film star, etc. who is at present in the news. Invent your name, nationality and details of your career, including the reasons for you being in the news, etc. Write brief notes to help you remember.

2 Work in pairs. Student A should pretend to be a journalist and should interview the 'famous' person (*ie*. Student B). Student A should note down the relevant, interesting details on his/her reporter's pad.

3 Now change roles and carry out a second round of interviews as in **2**.

G Writing

1 Write an article on the 'famous' person you have interviewed. Decide whether you are writing for a serious or popular newspaper and try to write in an appropriate style. Invent a suitable headline.

2 You want to become a journalist and decide to write a letter of application to a news agency. Include in your letter reasons for wanting the job and also why you think you would make a good journalist.

Unit 18   The Soap Opera

A1 'Soap Opera' is the name given to a radio or TV serial drama dealing with personal intrigues and domestic problems in a highly melodramatic and sentimental way.

Imagine that several proposals are being considered by the directors of a British TV company for a new serial that is scheduled to be shown in 8 hourly episodes, once a week at peak viewing time (8.30–9.30 pm).

Below is an outline sketch of the cast of characters in one of the proposed serials called 'The Family'. Read it carefully and draw a family tree showing the relationships between each character.

Proposal for TV Serial—'The Family'

The Cast:

Margaret Wilkins, a tough, matriarchal figure who worries about her children.

Marian Wilkins, 19, the elder daughter, works as a hair stylist and lives with Tom, an ex-steelworker from Sheffield.

Tom, 25, is reluctant to marry and lives with Marian in her parents' house. He is a colourful but rather worthless character who dislikes work of any sort.

Another room in the house is occupied by **Gary**, 18, the elder of the two sons and his wife, **Karen**, also 18. They married at 16 because Karen was expecting their son, Scott. Gary works as a bus conductor. Karen spends most of her time being taught the role of 'mother' by Mrs Wilkins.

Relations between Karen and **Heather**, 15, the Wilkins' second daughter are very bad. Heather's boyfriend, **Malvin**, is black and unemployed. Heather's resentment towards her sister-in-law is largely due to the fact that Karen and Gary occupy a room which she might have had; while she has to share a room with the youngest son, **Christopher**, aged 9. Christopher is the child of another man with whom Margaret Wilkins had a brief affair during a temporary breakdown of her marriage.

Terry Wilkins, 39-year-old bus driver and head of the family accepts the boy as his own.

---

2   Discuss your opinions about the above proposal with the rest of the class.

Do the characters seem to you credible or exaggerated and far-fetched?

Do you think that a serial based on this cast of characters is likely to be a success or not?

Do you think that the proposed name for the serial — 'The Family' — is likely to appeal to most viewers?

Do you think you would enjoy watching a serial of this kind?

69

B   Working in groups of 3 or 4, invent an outline plot for the proposed serial 'The Family' based on the description of the cast given above. Do not work out the detail of each week's programme, but rather the general story line that will develop through all eight episodes. Remember that 'The Family' is to be a soap opera and so you can make it as sentimental and melodramatic as you like!

C1   Now tell the rest of the class the outline plot your group has invented. After you have heard all the different versions, decide which one you think would make the most successful TV serial.
2   Discuss your opinions with the rest of the class and try to come to a consensus about which version of the plot you would choose if you were the directors of the TV company.

Ⓚ   **D1**   When you have chosen the best plot turn to page 180 in the Answer Key and read the notes.
2   Discuss the implications of what you have read on page 180 with your partner and the rest of the group. Use the following questions as a guide:
  1 What could the motives of the director be for making such a serial?
  2 What could the motives of the family be for participating?
  3 In what ways would the filming affect the family's life?
  4 Do you think the family could ever be really 'natural' in such circumstances?
  5 In what ways might the making of such a serial be socially useful or socially harmful?
  6 What might the effect be of making a similar serial in your own country?

E   Writing
Imagine that you have been contacted by an international TV Company and asked if you would be prepared to cooperate in a similar 'real-life' serial in your own country. The serial is one of several to be made for an international festival whose aim is to promote a better understanding between peoples of different nationalities and cultures.

Write a reply to the TV company, *either* accepting *or* rejecting their proposal and giving reasons for your decision.

Unit 19   Children and Television

Ⓚ **A1**   The article below is based on a recent survey to find out about children's TV viewing habits in Britain.

Read *paragraphs 1–5 only* and answer the following questions:

(*i*) What percentage of the nation's children view TV every day? _____

(*ii*) After what time are more violent and intimate scenes shown on TV? _____

(*iii*) What percentage of young children may sometimes view TV after 9 o'clock? _____

5–8 yrs	
9–11 yrs	

(*iv*) How many mothers in the survey said they allowed their children under 10 to watch anything they liked? _____

(*v*) What percentage of parents agreed or partly agreed that there was too much violence on TV? _____

(*vi*) How many thought sex on TV was more harmful than violence? _____

WATCHING WITH MOTHER
By Elkan Allan

Para 1   I am greatly concerned by the findings of a questionnaire to mothers about children's viewing habits, carried out for *TV Times*. I am not as surprised as European Marketing Surveys are by what they call the 'incredible amount' watched — 90 per cent of the nation's children viewing every day. What does worry me is the negligence revealed on the part of parents.

Para 2   Eight out of 10 children are 'usually or sometimes' allowed to watch right up to 'their bedtime'; a third of five to eight-year-olds and two-thirds of nine to 11-year-olds are allowed to stay up after their normal bedtime at weekends to watch TV.

Para 3   There is a notional 'watershed' at 9 pm, fixed by the BBC and IBA, after which more violent and intimate scenes can be shown and adult themes explored. But the survey reveals that 24 per cent of even five to eight-year-olds are sometimes allowed to view after nine o'clock, and half of the nation's nine to 11-year-olds may actually be watching then. As mothers could be expected to play down their estimates, 'the real figures would be even higher,' adds the author of the survey's summary.

Para 4   Only 62 out of the 524 mothers interviewed said they allowed their children under 10 to watch anything they liked. But implicit in the figures is that adult taste rather than concern for the child's mind is the main factor governing a decision to switch off (27 per cent) or switch over (57 per cent) when parents considered a programme unsuitable.

Para 5   Just two per cent stopped their children watching the violent *Starsky and Hutch*; only one per cent banned *The Professionals* or *Charlie's Angels*. The programme with the highest percentage — six out of a hundred — of parents forbidding it from the screen was one designed for children, *Dr Who*. Yet 74 per cent agreed or partly agreed that there was too much violence on TV. Interestingly, only eight per cent thought sex on television was more harmful.

Para 6   What emerges most clearly from the mass of figures is that parents exercise little or no control over their children's viewing, even when it worries them. They throw the onus on to the programme-makers, which is both cowardly and irresponsible. The people who make and schedule programmes should not be the ones who have to worry about little children being upset.

Para 7   Much as I am against any form of censorship, this survey convinces me that there should be some sort of indication given to parents as to the suitability of programmes. While children cannot be prohibited from viewing at home by anyone except their parents, as they can be by an 'X' certificate in the cinema, there is a precedent for guidance in another way. Adult American movies now carry an 'R' for Restriction Recommended. Adopting an 'R', to be clearly attached to tricky titles in programme journals and in on-air trailers, would be of immense assistance to responsible parents, and would encourage those who are less keen to take their job of guiding the young seriously.

Para 8   Personally, I would like to put an 'R' on all those nasty, smutty 'comedy' shows like *Benny Hill*, *Pig in the Middle*, and *George and Mildred*, but I realise that I might be letting my own prejudices carry me away, and this is always the danger with people who set themselves up as censors.

2   Check your answers with your partner. Discuss briefly which of the survey's findings you find interesting or surprising and explain why.

Ⓚ **3**   Now read *paragraphs 6–8* of the article and answer the following questions:

    (i) What main conclusion does the writer draw from the figures in the survey? _____

    _____

   (ii) What suggestion does he make?

    _____

    _____

  (iii) What is the danger of this?

    _____

    _____

4   Compare and discuss your answers with your partner and the rest of the group.

Ⓚ **B** **Vocabulary**

Find words in the article that have a similar meaning to the following:

    (i) failure to take proper care *(para 1)* _____

   (ii) theoretical, in name only *(para 3)* _____

  (iii) likes and preferences *(para 4)* _____

  (iv) responsibility *(para 6)* _____

   (v) problematic, difficult *(para 7)* _____

  (vi) short extract of a film used to advertise it in advance *(para 7)*_____

 (vii) indecent, obscene *(para 8)* _____

C   Discuss with the rest of the class your opinions about
   (i) the findings in the survey.
   (ii) Elkan Allan's worries.
   How far do you think the recommendation he makes would really make a difference in families where mothers, in particular, find the TV a very welcome presence in the home?

Ⓣ Ⓚ **D1**   You are now going to listen to a mother of 3 young children giving her opinions about TV and the way it affects her family's life. As you listen to the tape note down the advantages she mentions of having a TV.

Ⓣ **2**   Check the list you have made with your partner and the rest of the group. Listen to the tape again, if necessary.

E1   Discuss the advantages mentioned on the tape. Can you think of any others? Are there any disadvantages that were not mentioned?
2   In the light of the tape you have just listened to, do you feel you have a clearer understanding of why parents exert so little control over the TV viewing habits of their children (as revealed in the survey)?
   Discuss your opinions with the whole group.

F1   Role-play
Elkan Allan refers in his article 'Watching with Mother' to the 'incredible amount' of TV watched by young children. On the tape you have listened to the reasons for this from a mother's point of view.
   But does it really matter? Is it harmful and damaging for children to watch too much TV?
   Below and on the next page are five different opinions on this controversial issue. Work in groups of between 3 and 5 and assign *one* of the opinions to each member of the group.

> "TV may be a vital factor in holding a family together where there are, for example, economic problems and husband and wife seem at breaking point. The dangerous influence is surely no more than all of us are exposed to every day... in advertising, in the press."

> "Primary and secondary education have improved out of all recognition since the arrival of TV in the home and this is not only because of programmes designed for schools. Through TV a child can extend his knowledge and it provides vital food for his imagination."

> "TV passes on to children the corrupting values of a corrupt society. It's only a matter of time before we can give statistical evidence of how many criminals society has given birth to in front of the TV on Saturday night."

> "You can blame TV for the fact that children take longer to learn to read these days and barely see the point any more of acquiring the skill. In my opinion watching TV should be strictly confined to 'treats'."

> "In my opinion, TV totally stifles the creative imagination of the child and this can seriously affect him in later life..."

2 Spend a few minutes individually thinking of further arguments you will use to back up the opinion you have been assigned.

3 Now discuss the issue with other members of the group using the arguments you have prepared. Do your best to support those who share a similar point of view and to try and persuade those who don't agree with you that your point of view is right.

G Writing

Write an article for an educational magazine which sets out clearly all the possible arguments regarding the harmful effects TV may have on young children. Conclude the article by outlining your own position and explaining the reasons for this.

Unit 20 The Language of Advertising

Ⓚ **A1** Below is a list of techniques which advertisers commonly use to persuade us to buy their products.

1 Association of ideas	*6* 'Before and after'
2 Key words	*7* 'The camera never lies'
3 Guilt	*8* Repetition
4 'Science'	*9* Brand names
5 Expertise	*10* 'Keeping up with the Joneses'

Find out exactly what each of these techniques involves by reading the descriptions below and matching them correctly with one of the labels from the above list. Write your answers in the spaces provided.

(a) _____

Some products are advertised as having a remarkable and immediate effect. We are shown the situation before using the product and this is contrasted with the situation that follows its use. Taking a tablet for a headache in such advertisements can have truly remarkable results. For not only has the headache gone, but the person concerned has often had a new hair-do, acquired a new set of clothes and sometimes even moved into a more modern, better furnished house.

(b) _____

One thing reminds us of another — especially if we often see them together. These reminders are sometimes more imaginary than real: for some people snow may suggest Christmas, for others silver candlesticks may suggest wealth. The advertiser encourages us to associate his product with those things he thinks we really want — a good job, nice clothes, a sports car, a beautiful girl-friend — and, perhaps most of all, a feeling of importance. The 'image' of a product is based on these associations and the advertiser often creates a 'good image' by showing us someone who uses his product and who leads the kind of life we should like to lead.

(c) _____

Advertisements often encourage us to believe that because someone has been successful in one field, he should be regarded as an authority in other fields.

The advertiser knows that there are certain people we admire because they are famous sportsmen, actors or singers, and he believes that if we discover that a certain well-known personality uses his product, we will want to use it too. This is why so many advertisements feature famous people.

(d) _____

Maybe we can't always believe what we're *told*, but surely we must accept what we're actually *shown*. The trouble is that when we look at the photograph we don't know how the photograph was taken, or even what was actually photographed. Is that delicious-looking whipped cream really cream, or plastic froth? Are the colours in fact so glowing or has a special filter been used?

It is often difficult to tell, but you can sometimes spot the photographic tricks if you look carefully enough.

(e) _____

If you keep talking about something for long enough, eventually people will pay attention to you. Many advertisements are based on this principle.

If we hear the name of a product many times a day, we are much more likely to find that this is the name that comes into our head when the shopkeeper asks 'What brand?' We usually like to choose things for ourselves, but if the advertiser plants a name in our heads in this way he has helped to make the choice for us.

(f) _____

In this age of moon flights, heart transplants and wonder drugs, we are all impressed by science. If an advertiser links his claim with a scientific fact, there's even a chance we can be blinded by science. The question is simply whether the impressive air of the new discovery or the 'man-made miracle' is being used to help or just to hoodwink us.

(g) _____

Advertisers may try to make us want a product by suggesting that most people, or the 'best' people, already use it and that we will no doubt want to follow them. No one likes to be inferior to others and these advertisements suggest that you will be unless you buy the product.

(h) _____

The manufacturer needs a name for his product, and of course he looks for a name that will do more than just identify or label: he wants a name that brings suitable associations as well — the ideas that the word brings to mind will help sell the product.

(i) _____

Most advertisements contain certain words (sometimes, but not always, in bold or large letters, or beginning with a capital letter) that are intended to be persuasive, while at the same time appearing to be informative. In describing a product, copy-writers insert words that will conjure up certain feelings, associations and attitudes. Some words — 'golden', for example — seem to have been so successful in selling that advertisers use them almost as if they were magic keys to increase sales.

(j) _____

Advertisers may invoke feelings that imply you are not doing the best for those you love most. For example, an advertisement may suggest that any mother who *really* loves her children uses a certain product. If she does not, she might start to think of herself as a bad mother who does not love her family. So she might go and buy that particular product, rather than go on feeling bad about it.

2   Check and compare your answers with your partner.

B1   Discuss the different advertising techniques described with the rest of the class. Try to think of examples of advertisements you are familiar with in order to explain how each one works. Are there any other advertising techniques you can think of which are not in the list? If so, describe how they work and give examples of advertisements where you have noticed them being used.
2   Do you think that some techniques are more effective than others for advertising particular products? If so, which?
3   Do you think some techniques appeal more than others to certain age groups and types of people? If so, which?

C1   Look at the advertisements on the next page and discuss with your partner what technique or combination of techniques is used in each.

76

2 Compare and discuss your opinions with the rest of the group.

D1 Imagine that you are copy-writers for a free-lance advertising agency and have been given the following information about a new product that is shortly to be put on the market.

> Product no. 1294X Special Skin Lotion
>
> *Available* in tubes and jars.
> *Suitable* for all ages, sexes and skin-types especially those who lead active outdoor lives or are exposed to high levels of air pollution.
> *Aims* to revitalise the skin and prevent wrinkles.
> *How to use*: After washing, apply to the face morning and night.

The manufacturer has asked you to invent a brandname and write and design an advertisement for his new product. You are free to choose whatever advertising techniques you like, but the manufacturer has particularly stressed that he wants the advertisement to appeal to men as well as women.

2 Compare your advertisement with those designed by other groups in the class and decide, in the light of the manufacturer's request, which one you think is best.

E Writing

Write a letter to the manufacturer explaining why you recommend he should use the advertisement your class considers best to advertise his new product.

Unit 21   Consumer Discrimination

Ⓚ   **A**   Read the introductory article below and answer the following questions:
(i) Why is it difficult to make first-hand judgements of quality about a product?
(ii) What two appeals do advertisements make?

The importance of consumer discrimination in domestic life is clear. Indeed, the evaluation and selection of manufactured items — from soap powders to cars — is an inescapable part of life in today's society. But most people have little knowledge of the actual production of what they buy and are therefore unable to make first-hand judgements of quality. So where do ideas of value for money originate? On what basis do we discriminate between two comparable products? Ideally, judgement is based on the type and quality of materials, construction, performance, appearance and price. Often, however, first-hand knowledge of these factors is not available and we rely on advertisements.

The essence of advertising is persuasion. To use reasoned argument in order to persuade people to buy a particular product seems a valid form of propaganda and, indeed, could be expected to assist the process of discrimination. But the advertiser's concern cannot be solely to assist discrimination. His appeal is therefore rarely directed towards reason alone but also towards the more emotional responses that may be triggered by associating a product with the private hopes, fears, prejudices, and anxieties that beset the average human being. And if these appeals can be disguised within a reasoned argument, so much the better.

Ⓚ   **B1**   The British Code of Advertising Practice exists to protect the consumer from being deceived and misinformed by advertisements. Their slogan is:

> # "ALL ADVERTISEMENTS SHOULD BE LEGAL, DECENT, HONEST AND TRUTHFUL" ✓

and in their own advertisement they invite consumers to exercise discrimination and to report to the authorities any advertisements which do not fulfill their requirements.

On p. 79 are extracts from the *General Principles* on which the British Code of

Advertising Practice is based. Read them and underline what you think are the key words or phrases in each paragraph. The first two have been done for you.

General Principles

1. Advertisements should not contain statements or visual presentations <u>offensive to the standards of decency</u> prevailing among those who are likely to be exposed to them.

2. Advertisements should not be so framed as to <u>abuse the trust</u> of the consumer or <u>exploit his lack of experience or knowledge.</u>

3. Advertisements should not without justifiable reason play on fear.

4. Advertisements should not contain anything which might lead or lend support to acts of violence, nor should they appear to condone such acts.

5. All descriptions, claims and comparisons which relate to matters of objectively ascertainable fact should be capable of substantiation, and advertisers and advertising agencies are required to hold such substantiation ready for production without delay to the CAP Committee of the Advertising Standard Authority.

6. Advertisements should not contain any statement or visual presentation which, directly or by implication, omission, ambiguity, or exaggerated claim, is likely to mislead the consumer about the product advertised, the advertiser, or about any other product or advertiser.

7. Advertisements should not misuse research results or quotations from technical and scientific literature.

8. Consumers should not be led to overestimate the value of goods whether by exaggeration or through unrealistic comparisons with other goods or other prices.

9. All comparative advertisements should respect the principles of fair competition and should be so designed that there is no likelihood of the consumer being misled as a result of the comparison, either about the product advertised or that with which it is compared.

10. Advertisements should not unfairly attack or discredit other products, advertisers or advertisements directly or by implication.

11. Advertisements should be clearly distinguishable as such whatever their form and whatever the medium used. When an advertisement appears in a medium which contains news, editorial or programme matter it should be so designed, produced and presented that it will be readily recognised as an advertisement.

12. Advertisements should not, without justifiable reason, show or refer to dangerous practices or manifest a disregard for safety. Special care should be taken in advertisements directed towards or depicting children or young people.

13. Advertisements addressed to children or young people or likely to be seen by them, should not contain anything whether in illustration or otherwise, which might result in harming them physically, mentally or morally, or which exploits their credulity, their lack of experience, or their natural sense of loyalty.

2 Check with your partner that you have underlined the appropriate words and phrases.

Ⓚ **C1** Discuss with your partner and explain in your own words what you think the following phrases mean in practice. Use examples to help you clarify what you want to say.

    1 offensive to the standards of decency *(1)*
    2 play on fear *(3)*
    3 capable of substantiation *(5)*
    4 misuse research results or quotations *(7)*

2 Compare your opinions with the rest of the class.

D Which principles do you think are most important in protecting the consumers' rights?

Are there any points not mentioned here that you think should be included in the code?

Discuss your opinions with the rest of the class.

E Role-play

1 Work in groups of four. Two of you are members of the British Advertising Authorities Board and two of you are members of the public who want to make a complaint. The two members of the public should choose any advertisement from a magazine or newspaper and invent a complaint, *eg.* you have found the product does not conform to the claims in the advertisement.

2 The two members of the public should now express their complaint to the members of the board and put a case for banning the advertisement. The members of the board do not want to ban the advertisement as it has already been approved by the Advertising Authorities. They should try to placate and answer the complaint of the two members of the public. It may be useful to refer to the Advertising Code to do this.

F Writing

Find an advertisement and invent a complaint about it. Write a letter to the Advertising Authorities expressing your complaint and requesting that the advertisement should be banned.

Unit 22 A Change is as Good as a Rest

A1 For people who work at the same job 8 hours a day, 11 months of the year, holidays are very important. A holiday is the one time in the year when people feel they can relax and forget about the pressures and problems that are normally part of their lives.

Imagine that you are planning a two-week holiday. Look at the list below and indicate with a cross ($\times$) which type of holiday you think you would find most relaxing and enjoyable. (If the type of holiday you would most enjoy is not there, add it to the list.)

1 hotel
2 self-catering villa or apartment
3 coach tour
4 holiday camp
5 cruise
6 walking holiday
7 driving holiday
8 camping holiday
9 caravan holiday
10 pony-trekking holiday
11 winter sports holiday
12 _____
13 _____

2 Discuss with your partner the type of holiday you have chosen and explain why you think it would suit you best.

3 Now briefly discuss your choices with the rest of the class. How many of you have made the same choice? Is there any relation between the kinds of holiday you have chosen and the kinds of job you do? For example, have students with desk-bound jobs chosen very active holidays or vice versa?

Ⓚ **B1** Sometimes a holiday that has been planned very carefully and looked forward to very keenly, does not come up to expectations. In fact, holidays can quite often be disappointments and people may come back to work two or three weeks later not as refreshed and relaxed as they had hoped. At least part of the reason for this may lie in people choosing a holiday that is basically unsuitable for them. You are Ⓣ now going to listen to a tape in which a travel agent discusses the reasons for this and gives some general tips on how to plan a holiday which won't disappoint you.

Read through the questions below and write the answers in the spaces provided as you listen to the tape.

(i) Does the travel agent agree with the saying that 'a change is as good as a rest'? _____

(ii) What kind of holiday does he say would suit
  (a) a big store manager? _____
  (b) his wife? _____

(iii) What is the trap that many people fall into when choosing a holiday?
_____
_____

81

(iv) What two examples of this does the travel agent give?

Person	Holiday chosen

(v) Why would their choices be unlikely to give them a restful holiday?

(vi) What general tips are given about planning holidays?

Environment	
Children	
Money	

2 Check and compare your answers with your partner. Listen to the tape again if necessary.

C1 Discuss with the rest of the class your opinions about whether 'a change is as good as a rest'. What other tips can you think of to give someone planning a holiday? (If you consider questions of climate, clothes, food and drink, language and culture, it may give you some ideas.)
2 Did the type of holiday you chose in **A** represent a big change from the kind of life you lead normally? If not, would you now reconsider your opinion about the kind of holiday that would be most relaxing for you?

Ⓚ **D1** One of the reasons for choosing an unsuitable or disappointing holiday no doubt comes from believing too literally what the holiday brochures and travel advertisements tell us. Clearly, advertisers want to persuade us that their holiday is best! They may achieve an even greater effect with the kind of language they use in their brochures.

On the next page is an extract taken from a holiday brochure. The contents have not been altered but the name of the resort has been changed. Read it and then answer the questions.

THE SUNSHINE COAST

A garden overlooking the sea, where winter is almond blossom time. Beaches of soft golden sand. A warm, crystal-clear sea. The constant companionship of a sun that will get you really brown.

And that is the Sunshine Coast. A real international holiday centre. Where tourists from the world over find joy in living. Playing golf or tennis. Seeing shows at casinos. Going skin diving, rowing or sailing. Trying out their skill at water ski-ing or riding. Every day of the year. Because it is always holiday time on the Sunshine Coast.

The Sunshine Coast can offer you literally hundreds of beaches. Sheltered by red-hued cliffs. Backed by pinewoods. And also delightful villages with fretwork chimneys. Hills rolling away into the distance. Old buildings that speak of the past. Up-to-date tourist amenities—hotels, tourist villages, apartments, camping parks.

Come and discover the Sunshine Coast. Where the countryside retains its primitive beauty. And where all the towns with their cosmopolitan atmosphere are sure to get to you. With restaurants. Bars. Night clubs.

(i) Note the adjectives used which make the Sunshine Coast beaches sound specially attractive.

_____

_____

(ii) What is suggested about the weather and seasons on the Sunshine Coast?

_____

What phrases suggest this?

_____

_____

_____

(iii) From this description, what major contrast exists in the area of the Sunshine Coast?

_____

(iv) In what way does this contrast add to the appeal of the description?

_____

2 Compare and discuss your answers with your partner.

E Consider the general appeal of the holiday brochure extract you have read. Does it appeal to those who like:

— glamour
— a sophisticated night-life
— an active out-door life
— to get away from it all
— fashion

— a cosmopolitan society
— comfort
— reminders of the past
— peace and quiet

or a combination of these? If so, which?

Discuss your opinions first with your partner and then with the rest of the class.

83

F1   Role-play

Work in groups of four. Imagine that Pair A went to the Sunshine Coast last January and Pair B is considering going there for a holiday this winter.

2   Preparation for Role-play

    (i) Pair A: You were very disappointed by the Sunshine Coast as you read the holiday brochure before going and found the reality quite different.

        Spend a few minutes making a list of the reasons for your disappointment based on the brochure. *Eg.* The almond blossom *was* out in January, but it was quite cold and rained a lot while you were there.

    (ii) Pair B: You have read the holiday brochure and think that the Sunshine Coast sounds a lovely place to go in winter. However, you want to find out a bit more about it from your friends. Spend a few minutes thinking of questions you would like to ask them. Base your questions on the description in the brochure. *Eg.* Is the sea really warm in January?

3   Pairs A and B should now get together to talk about having a holiday on the Sunshine Coast. Pair B should ask questions and Pair A should warn them about what to expect.

G   Writing

1   Write a letter to a friend warning him/her against having a winter holiday on the Sunshine Coast (or any other place of your choice).

2   Write a description of your town or region for a new holiday brochure that is being written for English visitors. (NB. It would be better to write whole sentences rather than a list of phrases as in the holiday brochure description of the Sunshine Coast.)

You and Alternatives

23	Is Being Single Still out of Line?	*page* 86
24	Living Collectively Ⓣ	91
25	Getting Away from It All Ⓣ	93
26	The Pneu Wave	96
27	Vegetarianism	101
28	Schools with a Difference	106
29	Super Race?	111
30	Who's Afraid of the Silicon Chip? Ⓣ	115

Unit 23 Is Being Single Still out of Line?

A What can you imagine about these women's situations from the pictures?
What kind of life do you think they lead?
What are some of the advantages and disadvantages of their situation?
Discuss your opinions first with your partner and then with the rest of the class.

B1 The growth of feminism and the Women's Movement over the last 20 years or so has done a lot to change people's attitudes towards the different roles men and women have in society and in their relationships with each other. But no matter how enlightened these attitudes seem, many people may still consider it odd that a woman can reach her thirties without a husband and children. The article below asks the question 'Is being single still out of line?', and tries to answer it by looking at the situation of an individual woman, Sheila, who is in her mid-thirties and not married. Read the article through to get a general understanding and answer the following questions:
  (i) Why is Sheila celebrating?
  (ii) Why do people find Sheila's situation surprising?
  (iii) In what ways are Sheila's sisters different from her?
  (iv) What is Moira's problem?
  (v) What made Sheila feel lonely last Sunday night?

IS BEING SINGLE STILL OUT OF LINE?

A woman who can reach her thirties without the help of a husband and children still seems an odd fish to many people.

Para 1 Sheila bought herself a bottle of champagne and a miniature television set for her thirty-fifth birthday this year. The telly was a bit of a luxury—she had a perfectly good colour set in the sitting room—but it would be nice to watch a programme in the bath sometimes, or in bed, or to put it up on a kitchen shelf

86

when she was cooking. Anyway, she felt she should mark having reached her half-way mark to the three score and ten, unscathed.

Para 2 When she goes home to see her mother every two months the people in the village pity Sheila. She's the one 'who never married'. She's the bright-eyed girl (still very attractive, you know) who never found a man. She's an oddity, something that has to be defined a little, and explained. She was just as good-looking as Sarah and Moira, even better looking. Why was it that they found men so easily, and married in their twenties... yet Sheila is still single.

Para 3 It's not as if she were a furiously talented career woman either. One could understand somebody who was married to a challenging job. What's very irritating is that Sheila works in a big building society, a grade above secretary but several grades below manager. She has always worked there, and they gave her a loan to buy her flat but she doesn't talk about work much. It's a job which earns her money. It's not a wonderful exciting world in there. At best it's pleasant and not very taxing. At worst it's monotonous and petty. Once she leaves the office she forgets it.

Para 4 And it's not as if she hadn't had boyfriends when she was younger either. People in the village remember her at tennis parties, and cycling off on picnics. Even more popular than Sarah and Moira actually. And she takes such care of herself; her clothes are always smart and young, she could pass for twenty-five any day. Older than her two sisters but she looks

years their junior. Of course she never had to go through pregnancy and childbirth and looking after toddlers. No wonder she has that untired, almost untouched look.

Para 5 It's not only the people in the village. Her mother worries too. "I'd be so happy if you were settled," she says fairly often to Sheila. "But I am settled," Sheila protests, and ticks off her flat, her car, her pension scheme, her payments into a private health insurance scheme. Her mother sighs and says that Sheila knows what she means, she means *properly* settled.

Para 6 She is a mystery to her two younger sisters also. Sarah, thirty-two, mother of two, both at school now; Sarah's thinking of going back to work but she hates the thought of copy typing. She'd like to help run a boutique or an antique shop, and is waiting for the right kind of thing to turn up. Sheila comes to dinner in Sarah's suburban home about twice a year. If Sarah provides an extra man for the occasion, Sheila is charming to him. If not, she is still charming. She seems to love her niece and nephew. She remembers their birthdays and gives them things they like. Once every holiday she takes them to the cinema and a meal.

Para 7 Moira's marriage is not so happy. Not everyone knows this but Alan has another girl and he even has a child by her. But Alan doesn't want to break up anything and neither does Moira, aged thirty with twins aged five. So life goes on. Outward civilities are kept. Nobody is hurt too much. But Moira never thinks it would have been better not to have married. Being married is natural, being single is not. Sometimes being married has more pitfalls than people realise, but still ... well it's security and it's what people do. Moira occasionally envies Sheila's holidays abroad, and was pea-green when Sheila went to California. "I just saved twenty-five pounds a month," Sheila had said. As if everyone could do that. Moira couldn't save five pounds a month, and Alan has two families to support out of a very average salary.

Para 8   But nobody ever broods about Moira's life or Sarah's. Nobody wonders why Moira has dark rings around her eyes, why a healthy young woman has to have sleeping tablets and tranquillizers. Nobody sees any yawning loneliness ahead of Sarah whose children are busy at school, whose husband is busy in his office, and whose own house is clean by ten a.m. and a whole long day opens up ahead. No, they never speculate about the married sisters, the single one is what fascinates everyone.

Para 9   "Sometimes I wish that I had been married at nineteen to someone entirely unsuitable and divorced at twenty-one," says Sheila. "Then perhaps people would stop speculating about me. I'd appear normal and uninteresting again to them. I'm a bit tired of being regarded with a kind of patronising pity. What's worse, I can't actually say that I'm happy in my own lifestyle, or they'll think I'm compensating. If I say I actually like living by myself and choose that way above any other, they start thinking 'Aha, methinks she doth protest too much'. It's really Catch 22 isn't it?"

Para 10   She was quite happy to talk about being single (it made a nice change she said). Usually people were too embarrassed to mention it. She often felt as if she had a hideous disfigurement which people tried studiously to ignore. She would be totally prepared to discuss being single or married with anyone if it ever arose, but people were so ashamed for her at this great age, they never said anything serious. Only arch, insincere little remarks came her way.

Para 11   "I know we all act a lot of the time," said Sheila thoughtfully. "But why do you think people act so determinedly towards a spinster? I would have thought that liberation and the Women's Movement might have got us to the stage where an unmarried female is not an embarrassment. Long ago, when a woman had to have a dowry to marry a man, and there were no careers, it was different. Naturally an unmarried aunt or sister was a disaster then. She had to come and live in someone else's house and do the laundry or the flowers. It must have been terrible."

Para 12   We didn't discuss Sheila's sex-life or lack of it. But we did discuss loneliness.

Para 13   "Yes of course I'm lonely sometimes. Last Sunday night I was very lonely indeed. I was at a very nice supper party, great fun and easy-going. I didn't have much to drink because I was driving. I dropped a couple at their home and then came back here. I didn't feel like going to bed, so I sat and had a glass of wine and listened to music for a couple of hours . . . and I thought how much I'd like to have someone I trusted, someone with the same sense of humour that I could sit with and discuss the evening. I felt very lonely for about an hour, and then I remembered that hardly anyone has someone with exactly the same reactions, the same sense of humour ... or if they have, it doesn't work all the time. I reminded myself that I was no more lonely than one half of any couple who might have come home from an evening, one wanting to talk, the other wanting to go to bed or fill the dish-washing machine. So I laughed at myself and went to bed and slept like a log."

2 Check and compare your answers to the five questions above, first with your partner and then with the rest of the class.

Ⓚ **3** Now read the passage more carefully and make notes in the tables below about:

(i) Other people's attitudes towards Sheila:

people in the village *(para 2)*	pity
her mother *(para 5)*	
her sisters *(paras 6 and 7)*	
friends and acquaintances *(para 10)*	

(ii) Sheila's opinions and attitudes about:

her job *(para 3)*	Unexciting and undemanding but earns her money. At best, pleasant. At worst, petty and monotonous.
people's speculation about her *(para 9)*	
talking about being single *(para 10)*	
people's behaviour towards single women *(para 11)*	
loneliness *(para 13)*	

4 Check and compare your answers first with your partner, then with the whole class.

C1 Discuss with the rest of the class the different attitudes people have towards Sheila. Do you find them surprising? Would you expect to find similar attitudes in your own country?

2 Look at the notes you have made about Sheila's opinions and attitudes. What do they tell you about her personality?

D Vocabulary

Ⓚ **1** Find words in the passage that have a similar meaning to the following:

     (i) unusual or strange person *(para 2)*
     (ii) difficult, demanding *(para 3)*
     (iii) unimportant, trivial *(para 3)*
     (iv) unsuspected dangers *(para 7)*
     (v) very jealous *(colloquial)* *(para 7)*
     (vi) concentrates on the depressing aspects of *(para 8)*
     (vii) mischievous, playful *(para 10)*

Ⓚ **2** *(i)* 'unscathed' *(para 1)* means unharmed. What does it tell you about Sheila's attitude to marriage?

  (ii) Explain the difference between what Sheila and her mother understand by 'settled' *(para 5)*.

  (iii) Explain in your own words the phrase 'outward civilities are kept' *(para 7)*.

  (ii) An example of a 'Catch 22'* *(para 9)* situation: You have no experience and want a job. Employers tell you that to get a job you must have experience. But, in order to get experience, you must have a job....

     Explain what Sheila thinks is the 'Catch 22' of being single.

E You have now read the passage twice and are quite familiar with the contents. Do you think it was written by a man or a woman? What evidence can you find in the passage to support your point of view?

    Discuss your opinions with the rest of the class.

F What, according to the passage, is the answer to the question in the title? How far do you agree with the writer's opinion on this? Discuss your ideas with the whole class.

G Writing

1 Imagine that you have started working for the same building society as Sheila and have got to know her and like her quite a lot. Write a letter to a friend in your own country describing your new work colleague and what she has told you about her situation and other people's attitudes towards her.

2 Write a letter to an English friend of yours who is planning to come and live in your country. Outline in what ways he/she may find attitudes in general different. (Choose the things that seem to you most significant, *eg.* having long hair, drinking alcohol, etc.)

* 'Catch 22' is an expression that has become common-place since it was used as the title of Joseph Heller's best-selling novel (1961).

Unit 24 Living Collectively

Living collectively means sharing a home with a group of other people (not members of your family), who may be male or female, single or married. Children may also often form part of a collective household.

The members of a collective take joint decisions about the running of the home. They usually share their income or divide household expenses according to how much each person earns. Household chores and looking after the children are divided equally among the different members of the group.

A   Briefly discuss your opinions about living collectively. What do you think you would like or not like about living in this way?

B1   You are now going to listen to an interview with Judy Sheppard who lives in a collective. Judy discusses living collectively as an alternative possibility to marriage and the nuclear family. (NB. nuclear family=the primary social unit consisting of parents and children.)

Read through the following questions before you listen to the tape.

(i)   Who is the speaker thinking of particularly?
_____

(ii)   How can they benefit from living collectively?
(a) _____
(b) _____

(iii)   What 2 problems of living in a group are mentioned?
(a) _____
(b) _____

(iv)   How is a nuclear family different from living collectively?
_____

(v)   What are the main advantages of living collectively
(a) _____
(b) _____
(c) _____

(vi)   Does the speaker think of collective living as an alternative for married couples or as a system for single parent families?
_____

2   Now listen to the tape and write the answers to the questions above in the spaces provided.

3   Check and compare your answers, first with your partner and then with the rest of the class.

C   In explaining her ideas about collective living, Judy uses the phrases below (which are listed in the order in which they occur on the tape). Listen to the interview again. Identify each phrase as you hear it and explain what it refers to and what it means in the context of this discussion about living collectively.

Do *not* write your answers. Discuss your explanations for each phrase either with your partner or with the rest of the class.

91

(i) agreement to compromise	*(v)* semblance of independence
(ii) collective responsibility	*(vi)* share out menial household chores
(iii) channel of communication	*(vii)* pooling resources
(iv) supportive structure	*(viii)* emotional friction

D1 Role-play

Work in groups of 4 or 5. Imagine that you all live together in a collective household. Usually life is fairly happy and relaxed with everyone doing their share of the work. Recently, however, a problem has arisen with one member of the collective, Diana. Diana is 24 years old and separated from her husband. She has a two-year-old son, Sam, who also lives in the house.

Six months ago, Diana was made redundant from her job with a large publishing firm and has been getting more and more depressed ever since. She hardly helps at all in the running of the home and, because she is out of work, contributes very little financially. She also seems quite happy to leave looking after Sam to other people in the house. She has recently started going out with a new boyfriend, Ted, whom none of you like very much. He drinks a lot and has a habit of turning up at the house at any time of the day or night, whether he's been invited or not. All of you are getting very fed up with the situation and have decided to hold an informal meeting, while Diana is away for the week-end, to decide what to do.

2 Spend a few minutes thinking about what you would do in such a situation.

3 Now hold the informal meeting. Discuss the ideas and suggestions of every member of the collective. Then decide on a plan of action for when Diana returns to the house on Sunday night.

4 Compare your plan of action with other groups who have been considering the same problem. Explain and justify the decisions you have made.

E1 On the tape Judy mentioned 2 problems and 3 advantages of living collectively. Work in pairs and make a list of as many other problems and advantages as you can think of.

2 Judy referred to the nuclear family as being more structured in its hierarchy. In other words, the father is usually the breadwinner, the mother usually stays at home and the children are emotionally and financially dependent on their parents.

Make a similar list of the problems and advantages of being part of a nuclear family.

3 Now get together with another pair and discuss the different advantages and problems you have thought of about living collectively and in the nuclear family. How far are you all in favour of the same system?

4 Can you think of any other systems, either in your own country or anywhere else in the world, that might also provide a viable alternative to the nuclear family? Discuss your ideas with the rest of the class.

F Writing

1 Write a feature article on living collectively for a weekly magazine. Base your article on the interview you have listened to.

2 Imagine that you live in a collective. Write a letter to a friend of yours who is coming to stay, explaining how you organise and run your home.

Unit 25   Getting Away from It All

A1   It is not uncommon these days to hear of people who for a variety of reasons become so disenchanted with life in a big city that they decide to give up their jobs and make a fresh start somewhere in the country.

Mike and Teresa, a married couple interviewed on tape, have already taken the decision to move away from city life permanently.

What specific reasons do you imagine might have led them to this? Discuss your opinions with the rest of the class.

Ⓣ Ⓚ **2**   Read through the questions below and then listen to the interview with Mike and Teresa and answer the questions in the spaces provided.

1 Where are they living at present? _____

2 What are their jobs?

   Mike: _____

   Teresa: _____

3 Give the problems of working in town. _____

_____

4 How many years have they been in their present jobs?

   Mike: _____   Teresa: _____

5 What reasons do they mention for wanting to move from the city?

   Mike: _____

   Teresa: _____

6 What have they bought? _____

   Where is it? _____

7 What condition is it in? _____

8 What do they aim to do with it? _____

9 What are they most looking forward to? _____

10 What does each plan to do?

   Mike: _____

   Teresa: _____

11 What is their biggest worry? _____

12 What does Mike like about city life? _____

13 Why do they expect it to be hard to make new friends? _____

_____

14 How have Mike's parents reacted? _____

15 And Teresa's parents? _____

16 What problems of bringing up children in the country are mentioned?

_____

17 What has been the reaction of Mike and Teresa's friends? _____

_____

18 And what if their plans don't work? _____

Ⓣ **3**   Check and compare your answers with your partner. If you do not agree with each other listen to the tape again.

93

Ⓚ **B** Below are some of the words and phrases used in the interview. They are listed in the order in which they occur. Listen to the tape again, identify each word or phrase as you hear it and explain what each means in context.

    (i) ... *throw up* their jobs
    (ii) ... *commuting* into town
    (iii) ... very *wearing*
    (iv) ... something that has suddenly *cropped up*
    (v) ... it's *a shell*
    (vi) ... it's *just about liveable in*
    (vii) ... my experience *in the trade*
    (viii) ... we've got *our feet fairly well on the ground*
    (ix) ... they were just *on the doorstep*
    (x) ... they could *pop round the corner*
    (xi) ... we might even *see too much of them*
    (xii) ... what might you do if it doesn't *come off?*

Discuss your explanations for each word or phrase with your partner or with the rest of the class.

C1 Role-play

Mike and Teresa have bought a cottage in the country. The cottage, which faces south, is situated on a gentle slope overlooking a fertile valley. Other similar cottages are nearby. The walls of the cottage are made of local stone which has been plastered and whitewashed. All of them are thick, solid and generally in good condition. There are sloping tiled roofs. Two large trees are growing in the small garden, which is surrounded by traditional drystone walls.

The cottage is divided into two quite separate parts with no connecting doors — perhaps farm animals were once kept in the back part. The front part has two doors and two windows. The back is entered by a door on the left side of the cottage; there are no windows. An attractive feature of the cottage is the split levels: the smaller of the back rooms is 50 cms higher than the larger one and a step joins the two rooms; similarly the room on the extreme right of the front part is 50 cms lower than the rest of this part and again there is a step (NB. Both steps are marked on the plan of the rooms).

At present there is no running water or electricity but both are now easily available and will be installed.

The makeshift kitchen was the room on the right at the front. There has never been a bathroom.

Look carefully at the plans of the property as it is now:
    (i) the site of the cottage, garden and surrounding walls;
    (ii) the rooms;
    (iii) the front of the cottage.

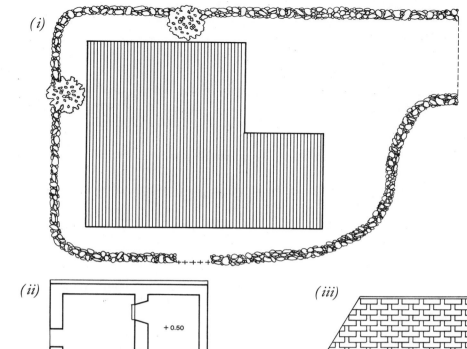

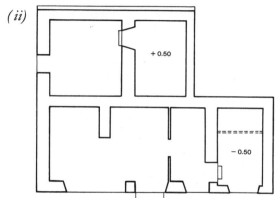

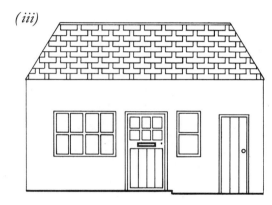

2 Work in groups of three or four. Imagine you are friends of the young couple and that you have offered your help in planning the changes that must be made to the cottage.

You must decide the arrangement of the following:

2 bedrooms	kitchen
sitting room	bathroom
dining room	fireplace(s) and chimney(s)

You should bear in mind the possibility of
  (i) removing some walls altogether
  (ii) making new internal and/or external doors and windows
  (iii) building a brand-new extension.

3 When you have finished explain to the other groups your ideas and justify your decisions.

Discuss and decide which group has made the best and most original proposals.

D Writing

1 Write a letter to the builder and explain and describe in detail the work you want him to carry out in order to convert and modernise your cottage.

2 Write a letter to a friend explaining that you have decided to give up your job and move to the country.

Unit 26 The Pneu Wave

Ⓚ **A1** More and more people in large cities throughout the world are finding it increasingly difficult, stressful and expensive to travel to the place where they work. Levels of air and noise pollution probably mean that it is bad for their health as well.

A solution to this problem may lie in using an alternative means of transport — the bicycle.

The article below is about commuting by bicycle in London. Read it and answer the questions that follow:

Para 1 As the cost and inconvenience of transport in the capital reaches ludicrous proportions, the arguments voiced by the cycling lobby become more and more compelling. For short-term commuting to and from central London, nothing can beat the bike; it keeps you in good shape, is quicker over relatively short distances and contributes nothing unpleasant to the atmosphere. Yet far from encouraging this effective means of transport the GLC* are extremely reluctant to consider anything put forward by the cycle groups, primarily proper parking facilities in central areas and around public buildings, and schemes for cycle ways. The saga of British Rail versus the bicycle continues with BR unwilling to allow space on trains for bikes being brought in and out of London during rush hour. In the meantime buses don't run, tube fares soar and cars containing one near apoplectic body jam the streets. Nevertheless last year sales reached an all time high as thousands of people discovered that travelling on a bike can be a highly pleasurable experience.

Para 2 The ideal way of deciding whether you could handle big city cycling is to hire a bike for a couple of days.

Para 3 Then you'll know if it's worth investing in a new or secondhand machine or whether you should emigrate to the countryside. Think carefully why you want a bike and what you are going to use it for.

Para 4 If you intend using a bike for short irregular journeys or for commuting less than five miles each way on a fairly level route, a roadster, usually with straight handlebars and three or five speed hub gearing is ideal. Minimum price £75. If your regular journey is over five miles each way, along a hilly or gradual incline route, or you plan to use the bike for a cycling holiday, then a derailleur with five or ten gears is best. Minimum price £85. Folding bikes are ideal for flat dwellers or families and have excellent luggage capacity. They adapt to most riders and are easy to manoeuvre; you can also take them on the tube. Their disadvantages are instability and the enormous effort required to cycle any distance—twice as much pedalling as a regular wheeled cycle. Minimum price £90.

*GLC = Greater London Council

(i) What are the advantages of using a bike in central London?

1	avoids cost and inconvenience of public transport
2	
3	
4	

(ii) What main changes in the present situation would cycle lobbies like to see?

1	
2	
3	

(iii) Fill in the chart with the information given about different kinds of bikes:

Type of bike	Cost	Suitable for
roadster (3–5 gears)		
	£85	
		flat dwellers or families

2 Compare and check your answers with your partner and the rest of the group.

Ⓚ **B Vocabulary**
Find words in the passage that have a similar meaning to the following:
    (i) forceful, convincing *(para 1)*
   (ii) group of people who try and influence those with power *(para 1)*
 (iii) long, eventful story *(para 1)*
 (iv) rise very quickly and steeply *(para 1)*
  (v) deal with, manage *(para 2)*

97

C1 The passage only mentions the advantages of commuting by bicycle in a large city. Work with your partner and make a list of the disadvantages *eg.* getting wet in the rain.

2 Compare and discuss with the whole group the advantages and disadvantages of commuting by bicycle in a large city.

Would you choose to go to work by bicycle if you lived in a large city? Explain the reasons for your answer.

Ⓚ **D1** If you answered 'no' to the last question, it is quite likely that one reason is that you are worried about the dangers of riding a bicycle in a large city, full of busy streets and congested traffic.

The following article gives some advice to cyclists on how to survive. For example, it suggests that you should familiarise yourself with the Highway Code, if you don't know it already. Look at the table below:

Highway Code	(re)familiarise yourself
Routes	
Position on Road	
Clothing	
Way to Ride	
Manoeuvres	
Rain	

Now read the article and complete the advice listed in the table.

STAYING ALIVE
A fairly important consideration

Para 1 Riding a bike in traffic will come as quite a shock if you've been used to any form of four wheels. From being relatively cocooned in a metal shell you are totally vulnerable on a bike and there is no dozing off. You will be using the roads in quite a different way and remembering this is particularly important if you also drive a car, so (re)familiarise yourself with the Highway Code. Get into the habit of planning your routes to avoid congested areas or fast main roads. Take up a position about an arm's length from the kerb, to avoid drain covers, pot holes, broken glass and so on. This is the safest position on the road and also gives you room to manoeuvre should a vehicle come too close.

Para 2 Although there are increasing numbers of cyclists on the roads, many drivers and pedestrians simply don't see a bike. Wear bright clothing or a fluorescent waistcoat and be positive: don't dither, ride in a straight line and learn to do so when looking behind. A right turn across oncoming traffic is one of the most hazardous exercises for a cyclist as you may have to stop in the middle to wait for a gap in the traffic. You'll feel less vulnerable if you can do this close to a bollard or island. Always plan such manoeuvres with care. It will make riding more pleasurable as well as safe.

Para 3 Try to anticipate every eventuality—car doors can suddenly open, pedestrians may pop out from behind a bus or truck. Be extra careful when it's raining: your brakes won't be as effective and other road users may be similarly hampered. All this will become second nature after a while but when riding a bike in a large city, you should always be careful and on your guard.

2 Check and compare the notes you have made with your partner.

E Vocabulary

Work with your partner. Discuss and help each other as much as you can.

1 The following items are illustrations of words taken from the passage and can be found in most urban streets. What are they? (Refer to the passage to help you answer.)

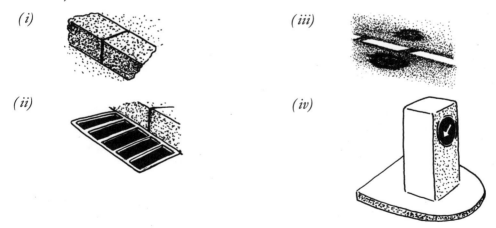

2 Explain these words and phrases as they are used in the passage in your own words:

  (i) cocooned in a metal shell *(para 1)*
  (ii) dozing off *(para 1)*
  (iii) dither *(para 2)*
  (iv) pop out *(para 3)*
  (v) hampered *(para 3)*

3 Now discuss your explanations with the whole class.

F1   Role-play

Work in pairs. Imagine that you both live and work in a large city. Student A already commutes by bicycle and feels that life would be much more pleasant if everyone did the same. Student B lives about 3 miles from his/her place of work and is considering buying a bicycle, but is not sure what kind would be best. He/she is also rather anxious about the dangers of riding a bike in busy traffic and wants to ask student A for advice.

2   Use the information tables in **A** and **D** to discuss the problem. Student B should ask as many questions as possible and student A should give advice. Student A should try and convince his/her partner that changing to using a bicycle would be best.

G   Writing

1   Imagine that you are a member of the cycling lobby in your town. You are organising a campaign to try and convert commuters to using bicycles to go to work. You have been asked to write the front page article of the campaign leaflet which should outline all the advantages of using bicycles in a large city.

2   A friend of yours who will shortly be moving to London is considering buying a bicycle to get around. He/she has written to ask your advice about whether this is a sensible idea. Write your reply.

Unit 27 Vegetarianism

A Food is something that is of immediate concern to everyone everywhere. It is also almost infinite in its variety.

The passage below considers some aspects of vegetarianism and compares the nutritional value of this way of eating with a normal mixed diet.

Before you read the passage briefly discuss your opinions about vegetarianism with the rest of the class. Use the following questions as a guide:

(i) Why do you think some people are vegetarian?

(ii) Do you think a vegetarian diet is less healthy than one which contains fish and meat?

(iii) Is any member of the class a vegetarian? Ask them to explain their personal views.

Ⓚ **B1** Now read the passage and fill in the table below.

Para 1 Meat, poultry and fish were not originally part of man's diet. Our teeth evolved to deal with tubers and seeds, not flesh. Our digestive systems are those of foragers, not hunters. We cannot gorge ourselves on meat and then go without eating for days as many carnivores do.

Para 2 Such evolutionary arguments may seem a thin basis for adopting a vegetarian diet today, however. The fact is that meat is a highly concentrated form of nutriment. It is also among the most appetizing foods in the average diet. Its flavours and smells are so thoroughly woven into the traditional Western way of eating that many people find the prospect of doing without it disheartening. Yet the evidence is that vegetarianism as a matter of individual choice is now spreading. For a variety of reasons, a habit that was once regarded as an eccentricity is gaining respect.

Para 3 A vegetarian diet may be adopted for any one of three reasons—the philosophy of the individual, the range of foods that are available locally, or the religious beliefs of a particular community. Religions can impose varying degrees of vegetarianism. The Ethiopian Coptic Church, for example, prohibits meat on more than 200 days of the year. Trappist monks abhor the taking of life and are entirely vegetarian. Of the major world religions, both Hinduism and Buddhism have similar objections to exploiting other living creatures for food. Strict followers of these faiths are wholly or partly vegetarian.

Para 4 A form of enforced vegetarianism is common in many parts of Africa and Asia, where meat costs so much to produce that poorer people are seldom able to eat it. About eighteen per cent of the world's population (excluding China) eat less than 10 g (0.3 oz) of animal protein per head per day—equivalent to two small eggs or one cup of milk.

Para 5 But with the spread of affluence, the amount of animal protein eaten in the average diet has been increasing. Vegetarianism

101

in the West is therefore less a matter of economic necessity than of choice. The number of voluntary vegetarians in Europe and the US is estimated at several million. Some are motivated by aesthetic or moral ideas; they deplore the killing of animals and some of the methods of raising them for food. Some base their choice on economics; it is more efficient to use land for growing food directly than for feeding animals. Still others simply believe a vegetarian diet is more healthy.

Para 6 An extreme form of vegetarianism is veganism. The Charter of the Vegan Society says that 'Veganism is a way of living which excludes all forms of exploitation of, and cruelty to, the animal kingdom and includes a reverence and compassion for all life'. In practice the vegan excludes from his diet not only meat, poultry and fish but also animal milk and other derivatives such as eggs and honey. Soya-based plant-milks are substituted for cow's milk and are equally nutritious. Extending the vegan philosophy to clothing, vegans use plastic, rubber and PVC instead of leather jackets, belts or shoes. Another well-known form of vegetarianism is the Zen macrobiotic diet, which originated in Japan and has been adopted in the West on a small scale in protest against the industry that has created 'bad' unnecessary foods. Certain foods are designated Yin and others Yang (an acid-alkaline contrast), and the dietary regime consists mainly of seven diets in which these foods are balanced. The 'ideal' diet is one of brown rice only, but it has been condemned by the American Medical Association as one of the most dangerous, since not only could it give rise to ill-health from malnutrition, but it could also lead people to avoid medical treatment because of the claims that it cures diseases (even cancer).

Para 7 But the special features of veganism and Zen macrobiotics aside, just how nutritious can a vegetarian diet be? In poorer countries it is often accompanied by general shortage of food and assessment is therefore difficult. In affluent countries, however, research shows that a vegetarian diet can be nutritionally sound for all ages, differing from a normal diet only in the sort of foods supplying the essential nutrients. Vegetables, fruits and nuts are excellent sources of the vitamins and minerals man needs and vegetarians tend to have relatively higher intakes of calcium, vitamin B, and vitamin C than people following a mixed diet.

Para 8 Since the quality of mixed cereal and certain vegetable proteins matches that of meat and fish proteins, vegetarian diets have protein values similar to those of mixed diets, provided adequate quantities are consumed. There is certainly a tendency for vegetarians to have lower Calorie intakes than people on mixed diets. This is largely because their fat intake is lower—an advantage in view of the association of high fat consumption with heart disease.

Para 9 The lower energy content of vegetarian diets requires some adjustments in total food intake. For instance, to provide 2,700 Calories (the recommended intake for an adult man) a person would need to eat 6 kg (13 lb) of apples, or 11 kg (24 lb) of raw cabbage or 1.1 kg (2.5 lb) of wholemeal bread. Vegetable foods tend to have a higher water content so that vegetarians automatically take larger quantities of water as part of their food, instead of additional liquid. Vegetables also have a lower fat content. However, if fat is required nuts are more than fifty per cent fat, oils can be added to salads and vegetable fats can be used in cooking.

Para 10 If, for whatever reason, you decide to give up meat, it does not mean that you will have to face a dull diet, existing on endless meals of tasteless and textureless vegetables. Vegetarianism is an alternative that can offer a surprisingly tasty and varied diet—and save money as well. Cheap foods such as flour, oatmeal, potatoes, haricot and broad beans, soya, carrots and spinach provide between them enough key nutrients to meet everyone's daily needs and more.

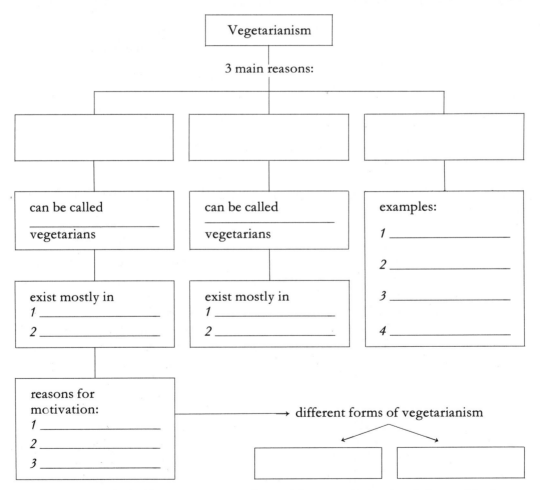

2 Compare and check your answers first with your partner and then with the rest of the class.

103

Ⓚ **3** Read paragraphs 8 and 9 again carefully. Complete the table below to show the sources of essential nutrients in a vegetarian diet and how the average intake of these compares with people following a mixed diet.

Nutrients	Intake in Relation to a Mixed Diet	Source
Calcium Vitamins B and C	higher	vegetables, fruit and nuts
Proteins		
Water		
Fat		

4 Check and compare your answers with your partner.

Ⓚ **C Vocabulary**

Find words or phrases in the passage which have a similar meaning to the following.

    (i) eat greedily, fill oneself *(para 1)*
    (ii) nourishing food *(para 2)*
   (iii) strange behaviour, abnormality *(para 2)*
   (iv) wealth, abundance *(para 5)*
    (v) express regret for and disapproval of *(para 5)*
   (vi) component of food, *eg.* vitamin which provides nourishment *(para 7)*

D Discuss your opinions about vegetarianism with the rest of the class. Use the questions below as a guide:

    (i) How far did your answers to questions *(i)* and *(ii)* in **A** correspond to what the passage says?
   (ii) Has the passage convinced you that a vegetarian diet can be just as healthy as one with meat and fish?
  (iii) What's your opinion about vegan or Zen macrobiotic diets? Would you consider such diets dangerous to health or not?
  (iv) Do you think vegetarianism means endlessly eating dull food? Or do you agree that vegetarianism can provide a tasty and varied diet?
   (v) How do you feel about becoming a vegetarian? Can you imagine deciding never to eat fish or meat again?

E1 Role-play

Look again at the table in **B** above which shows the different reasons for adopting a vegetarian diet. You will notice that 'voluntary vegetarianism' exists principally in the affluent countries of the West whereas 'enforced vegetarianism' is a feature of poorer countries.

In the affluent countries there is a very great variety of different kinds of food which, generally speaking, people can afford to buy if they want to. Just think of the convenience packaged foods available on the shelves of any supermarket, for example! It is in this context, although for various different reasons, that most vegetarians living in wealthy western countries choose to follow a particular diet. In poorer countries, most vegetarians do not have the luxury of making such a choice and it may often be a matter of eating anything that is available in order to survive. The continuing increase in the population, particularly in the countries of Asia, Africa and Latin America, make food shortage a problem which is likely to become more acute in the future. Added hazards, such as droughts or insect blights which may destroy a whole crop at any one time make it even more urgent that an international solution to the problem of world food distribution should be found.

2 Work in groups of 3 or 4. Imagine that you are members of an advisory committee to an international agency similar to the United Nations. You are meeting to discuss ways in which the governments of more affluent countries can cooperate internationally to help avert a world food crisis. Below are some outline proposals that have been submitted for your consideration:

> *1* Governments should organise a system for the emergency distribution of food to poorer countries in case of crop failure, drought, etc.
>
> *2* Governments should sell their own surplus foodstuffs to poorer countries at very reduced prices.
>
> *3* Governments should actively discourage the cultivation of crops like tobacco which take up valuable agricultural space and do not contribute to the world supply of nutriments.

3 Each member of the Advisory Committee should individually think of *one* more proposal to take to the meeting.

4 The Advisory Committee should now meet and one of the members should act as chairperson. You should discuss all the proposals in turn and decide whether to recommend that they should be adopted or not.

In your discussion you will need to consider such things as the willingness of individual governments to agree to the proposals and to work out some general ideas as to how the proposals you would like to adopt might be put into practice.

5 Each group should now report on their discussion and decisions to the rest of the class. How far do you agree on the three proposals considered by all the groups?

How many new proposals has each group decided to adopt? What are they?

6 Try to come to an agreement with the whole class about any five proposals which you would like to recommend to the International Agency for their further consideration. Try and convince other members of the class that the proposals you would like to recommend are the best ones.

7 If, after discussing all the proposals, you cannot agree, take a vote on each proposal in turn. Each member of the class has five votes.

F Writing

1 As a member of the Advisory Committee, write a letter to the International Agency recommending the five proposals which you think would help to avert a world food crisis. Explain fully your reasons for recommending each proposal.

2 Write a report on the three main types of vegetarianism for an international current affairs magazine. Base your article on the information in the table in **B**.

105

Unit 28 Schools with a Difference

Most people have strong opinions about the kind of schools they went (or go) to. Often this is a result of their own personal experiences which leave them feeling that there is much to criticise and little to praise in the kind of schooling they received. How many people in your class, for example, have bad memories of things that happened to them at school?

But just what are the alternatives to the conventional school?

Ⓚ **A1** Summerhill is a boarding school with a difference. Founded in 1921 by the late A. S. Neill, it is situated in Suffolk, England, about 100 miles from London. Although begun more than 60 years ago, Summerhill still represents an experiment in education that is unique of its kind.

Look at the chart which gives information about various features of an ordinary boarding school. Then read the extract from A. S. Neill's book *Summerhill* and note in the spaces provided the information that makes Summerhill different from an ordinary boarding school.

	Ordinary Boarding School	Summerhill School
Sleeping quarters	Dormitories	
Clothes	School uniform	
Discipline	Likely to be a lot	
Moral and religious instruction	Obligatory	
Lessons	Obligatory	
Teaching methods	Usually believed that teaching methods affect rate of learning	
Examination performance	12-year-olds likely to do well in handwriting, spelling, etc.	
Truancy	On the increase	
Relation between teachers and pupils	Teachers are usually figures of authority	

106

Para 1 Summerhill was founded in the year 1921. The school is situated within the town of Leiston, in Suffolk, and is about one hundred miles from London.

Para 2 Some children come to Summerhill at the age of five years, and others, as late as fifteen. The children generally remain at the school until they are sixteen years old. We generally have about twenty-five boys and twenty girls.

Para 3 The children are housed by age groups with a housemother for each group. Most pupils live two or three or four to a room; only one or two older ones have rooms for themselves. The pupils do not have to stand room inspection and no one picks up after them. They are left free. No one tells them what to wear: they put on any kind of costume they want to at any time.

Para 4 When my first wife and I began the school, we had one main idea: *to make the school fit the child*—instead of making the child fit the school. We set out to make a school in which we should allow children freedom to be themselves. In order to do this, we had to renounce all discipline, all direction, all suggestion, all moral training, all religious instruction.

Para 5 My view is that a child is innately wise and realistic. If left to himself without adult suggestion of any kind, he will develop as far as he is capable of developing. Logically, Summerhill is a place in which people who have the innate ability and wish to be scholars will be scholars; while those who are only fit to sweep the streets will sweep the streets. But we have not produced a street cleaner so far. Nor do I write this snobbishly, for I would rather see a school produce a happy street cleaner than a neurotic scholar.

Para 6 What is Summerhill like? Well for one thing, lessons are optional. Children can go to them or stay away from them—for years if they want to.

Para 7 The children have classes usually according to their age, but sometimes according to their interests. We have no new methods of teaching because we do not consider that teaching in itself matters very much. Whether a school has or has not a special method for teaching long division is of no significance, for long division is of no importance except to those who *want* to learn it. And the child who *wants* to learn long division *will* learn it no matter how it is taught.

Para 8 Children who come to Summerhill as kindergarteners attend lessons from the beginning of their stay; but pupils from other schools vow that they will never attend any beastly lessons again at any time. They play and cycle and get in people's way, but they fight shy of lessons. This sometimes goes on for months. The recovery time is proportionate to the hatred their last school gave them. Our record case was a girl from a convent. She loafed for three years. The average period of recovery from lessons aversion is three months.

Para 9 All the same, there is a lot of learning in Summerhill. Perhaps a group of our twelve-year-olds could not compete with a class of equal age in handwriting or spelling or fractions. But in an examination requiring originality, our lot would beat the others hollow.

Para 10   Summerhill is possibly the happiest school in the world. We have no truants and seldom a case of homesickness. We very rarely have fights—quarrels, of course, but seldom have I seen a stand-up fight like the ones we used to have as boys. I seldom hear a child cry, because children when free have much less hate to express than children who are downtrodden. Hate breeds hate, and love breeds love. Love means approving of children, and that is essential in any school. You can't be on the side of children if you punish them and storm at them. Summerhill is a school in which the child knows that he is approved of.

Para 11   In Summerhill, everyone has equal rights. No one is allowed to walk on my grand piano, and I am not allowed to borrow a boy's cycle without his permission. At a General School Meeting, the vote of a child of six counts for as much as my vote does.

Para 12   But, says the knowing one, in practice of course the voices of the grownups count. Doesn't the child of six wait to see how you vote before he raises his hand? I wish he sometimes would, for too many of my proposals are beaten. Free children are not easily influenced; the absence of fear accounts for this phenomenon. Indeed, the absence of fear is the finest thing that can happen to a child.

2   Check and compare what you have noted in the chart with your partner and the rest of the class.

Ⓚ   **B   Vocabulary**

1   Find words or phrases in the text which have a similar meaning to the following:

    (i)   tidies, clears up for *(para 3)*
    (ii)   oppressed, treated badly *(para 10)*
    (iii)   shout angrily *(para 10)*

2   Explain what the following words and phrases mean from the context in which they are used:

    (i)   loafed *(para 8)*
    (ii)   fight shy of *(para 8)*
    (iii)   beat the others hollow *(para 9)*

C   Discuss Summerhill with the rest of the class. Use the following questions as a guide:

    (i)   How does Summerhill differ from the kind of school you went (go) to?
    (ii)   What features of the school do you like?
    (iii)   What features of the school don't you like?
    (iv)   Is there any feature that makes you doubt whether a school like this can really work?
    (v)   Do you think you would (benefit) have benefited from going to a similar school? If so, in what ways?
    (vi)   Would you send your child to a school like this? (Think out the reasons for your answer carefully.)

D Writing

1 Write a comparison *either* between Summerhill and an ordinary boarding school based on the information in the table *or* between Summerhill and a school you know through personal experience.

2 Imagine that a friend of yours is considering sending his/her child to Summerhill. Write a letter either encouraging or discouraging him/her.

E1 Another alternative in education — the City-as-School — has been started in New York, USA. Below is an article about the school. Before you read it, try and predict from the name, what kind of schooling it might provide and discuss your ideas with the rest of the class.

2 Now read the article to find out how accurate your predictions were.

The City-as-School idea itself is not new but the New York programme is generally recognised as being the most successful of its kind.

Three hundred and fifty high school students between 15 and 18 attend the City-as-School: it's a school without walls and its 'classroom' is the city itself. Students spend their days in the theatres, museums, government offices and businesses of New York in a programme of part-time apprenticeships that are individually tailored to their interests and needs.

Pam Bruno, 16, for example, spends part of her time in the City Council press office, finding out about New York politics as she helps prepare press releases and assists in the running of the office. Another day is spent at New York University where she takes first year courses in sociology and 'main themes in contemporary world history'. She also works for a Women's Centre, travelling about the City interviewing women in business for a report that's soon to be published. Yet another day is spent at a television casting agency, learning what show business is all about.

Students are accepted into City-as-School after an interview; the only academic requirement is two years of basic mathematics and science at a high school.

Credits are given, for satisfactory completion of each assignment, so that the students stand as good a chance of getting into an American college as their counterparts in ordinary high schools. In fact it was shown recently that 80–85 per cent of CAS graduates are going on to college without problems.

As might be expected, many of the CAS students are young people who, for one reason or another, were unhappy with conventional education. Pam Bruno dropped out of the conventional system because she was bored: 'I felt stifled by an educational system that didn't seem to care about me. I was just a number.'

The New York City-as-School is viewed as a useful alternative way of dealing with these final and often troublesome school years. There are, however, still some lingering doubts as to whether this kind of 'Life experience' can totally replace the academic development acquired in a classroom.

F Is this the first time you have heard of such a school? Discuss your reactions with the rest of the class.

In your discussion consider the advantages of this kind of education as a preparation for later life as opposed to more conventional schooling.

G1   Work in groups of 3 or 4. Imagine that the town in which you live (or study) is planning to set up a similar City-as-School. Work out six projects for students to do in the town which you think will be of value to them in later life, *eg.* helping in the offices of the local newspaper, working in the local town hall, etc.

2   Compare the six projects you have worked out with those of other groups.

Discuss and decide the six best projects from among all those worked out in the class.

H Writing

Write a letter to someone in your town who you would like to be involved in the City-as-School project, *eg.* editor of the local newspaper. Outline the aims of the school and ask for his cooperation in being involved in one of the student projects.

Unit 29   Super Race?

A   Look at the news headline and explain what it means in your own words. How far does it help you to predict the content of the news article?

**NOBEL SPERM BANK CREATOR
DENIES GOAL OF ELITE RACE**

Discuss your ideas with the rest of the class.

B1   Now read the news article and see how accurate your predictions were. Find the answers to the following questions:
  (i)   How does Mr Graham justify what he's doing?
  (ii)   What has the general reaction of Nobel scientists been?
  (iii)   What does Dr Shockley think?

From Ivor Davis
Los Angeles, March 2

The California optometrist who has been criticized for starting a sperm bank containing donations from only Nobel Prize-winning scientists, says that creating a master race was not his intention. He disagreed with comparisons between what he is doing and the Nazi theories of building an elite.

"I don't know that much about Hitler and his vision," Mr Robert Graham said to journalists in the garden of his 10-acre property, "but I don't see any parallel. We are not thinking of a super race, we are thinking in terms of a few more creative, intelligent people who otherwise would not be born."

In fact, Mr Graham said, he hoped that sperm banks would be started for "Olympic gold medallists, artists, or movie stars'."

He said he began soliciting Nobel scientists' sperm in 1977, for the "Hermann J. Muller Repository", named after the 1946 winner of the Nobel Prize in medicine, who died at the age of 76 in 1967 and had strong views on the declining endowment of the human race.

The bank provides sperm at no cost to women who are young, married, of high intelligence, and whose husbands are infertile. So far, Mr Graham said, three women have been inseminated, though it is not known if they are pregnant, and "several dozen women around the country have expressed an interest in following suit."

The Los Angeles Times reported today that of 23 Nobel scientists contacted, 11 of them said they had been called by Mr Graham. All but Dr William B. Shockley of Stanford University, who shared the 1956 Nobel Prize for physics, said they had turned down the request.

Dr Shockley, aged 70, said that the repository was a remarkable attempt, and "I'm thoroughly in sympathy with this sort of approach." The scientist, controversial for his genetic theories of intelligence, said he was disappointed that more of his fellow Nobel scientists had not been willing "to add their names to this good cause."

Dr Max Delbruck, winner of the 1969 prize in physiology, said: "I think it's pretty silly."

At the Salk Institute in La Jolla, California, Dr Robert Holley, who took the prize for medicine in 1969 and turned down Mr Graham's invitation to donate sperm, said: "What surprises me is that any woman would want this. But I guess people are entitled to do what they want."

111

2 Now check your answers to the three questions with the rest of the class.

C Discuss your reactions to the sperm bank project with the rest of the class. How far do you agree with Dr Holley that 'people are entitled to do what they want'? Of, do you think there should be legislation to forbid this kind of experimentation?

Ⓚ **D1** The moral questions raised by the creation of the sperm bank have turned it into an extremely controversial issue. On the day the news article you have read appeared in *The Times*, there was also an editorial which considered some of the main arguments surrounding the subject. Read the editorial comment carefully and underline what you consider are the main points in each paragraph. (You should find *one* main point in paragraphs 1–5 and *three* in the last paragraph).

CALIFORNIA'S GERMINAL BRAINS BANK

Para 1 The project to breed a race of intellectual giants out of a lead-lined box in California need not fill mankind with any very extreme hopes or fears. The idea forms an obvious starting-point for a variety of science fiction fantasies, but in practice it is unlikely to add greatly to the world supply of brain-power, nor shed much light on the vexed question of intellectual inheritance. Most Nobel prizewinners and their equivalents already make their own private arrangements for passing their genes to posterity, and since like tends to attract like in such matters, they must often choose partners of high intelligence. But the mechanism of inheritance is such that their offspring are likely on average to be less intelligent than their parents, though more so than the average. The same rules will apply to the Nobel mothers too.

Para 2 The appearance of really exceptional powers remains unpredictable and highly improbable in any given instance. The successful application of such powers to the advancement of human knowledge or welfare is even more a matter of chance and temperament. It is possible to cite extraordinary cases of talent being passed down from generation to generation (the Bach family is one), but easy to cite many other instances where it has not.

Para 3 It would be pleasing if we could look to the experiment to illuminate the old "nature versus nurture" controversy, but so many imponderable factors creep in that the conclusions are never likely to be at all clear. Even strong proponents of the "nature" doctrine usually concede that environmental factors can affect measured intelligence by as much as one-fifth—and 20 or 30 points on the IQ scale span the difference between genius and mediocrity.

Para 4 But if the scheme affords no promise of a team of infant sages to solve the world's problems, it appears, on the information so far made public, to present no special ethical problems. Genetics is a field where academic passions run high, but it would be wrong

112

to oppose the procedure out of opposition to the views on heredity of some of those associated with it. The scheme is freely entered into by participants who know what they are doing. The expectant mothers are married and able to offer their children the benefits of a secure home.

Para 5 The plan does raise some questions, however, which do not apply to artificial insemination by donor generally. Success in the Nobel stakes is as closely associated with advancing years as it is with intellectual eminence, and this may involve a very slight extra risk of miscarriage or congenital abnormality—a point which should be made in preliminary counselling. The children would represent an interesting object of study, and care would have to be taken to ensure that they did not become afflicted with a sense of obligation to succeed, and cry with Aldous Huxley, "Shame on you, Homunculus!"

Para 6 It seems that the mothers in this case have not been told the identities of the donors, though they know some details about them. That is right: it would be distasteful if a market—especially a commercial one—ever established itself in the genes of famous individuals (pop stars, perhaps, as well as professors). No one donor should be used too often, however eminent, because of the risk of marriages between unwitting half-brothers and sisters. AID today is widely practised and causes little controversy, because there is reason to suppose that the medical profession handles it responsibly. The California experiment, though not seriously objectionable in itself, indicates the kind of developments which might lead to increased concern and demands for regulation by law.

2   Check with your partner and the rest of the class that you agree on the main points of each paragraph.

Ⓚ **E   Vocabulary**
1   Find words in the editorial that have a similar meaning to the following:
   (i)   to give example of *(para 2)*
   (ii)   allows for *(para 4)*
   (iii)   suggestions and advice *(para 5)*
   (iv)   unaware *(para 6)*
   (v)   well-known, respected *(para 6)*
2   Explain these phrases in your own words.
   (i)   shed much light on the vexed question of intellectual inheritance *(para 1)*
   (ii)   'nature versus nurture' controversy *(para 3)*
   (iii)   where academic passions run high *(para 4)*
   (iv)   success in the Nobel stakes *(para 5)*

Ⓚ **F1   Writing**
Write a summary of the editorial article using the main points in **D1** and the table on the next page as a guide. Look carefully at the example before you begin.

113

Example: *Paragraph 1*: The California Brains Bank is unlikely to add greatly to the world supply of brain-power, since (because/as) offspring are likely on average to be less intelligent than their parents.

Paragraph	Connector	Connecting
1	since/because/as	main point to subsidiary point
2	although	main point to subsidiary point
3	in addition/moreover	Paragraph 2 to Paragraph 3
4	but	Paragraph 3 to Paragraph 4
5	however	Paragraph 4 to Paragraph 5
6	(1) (no connection needed) (2) also/moreover (3) in conclusion	Paragraph 5 to Paragraph 6 main point to main point main point to conclusion

2 Check and compare the summary you have written with your partner's and then with the rest of the class.

G Discuss briefly what you consider is the general attitude of the editorial towards the sperm bank project. Would you describe it as impartial and objective or can you detect a bias in the way the arguments are developed?

H Writing
In response to the news article and editorial, write a letter to *The Times* putting forward your own point of view on the sperm bank scheme.

I Role-play
1 Work in groups of 4–5. Imagine that you are on the editorial board of *The Times* and are going to choose 3 of the many letters you have received about the sperm bank scheme to publish in tomorrow's paper. Read the letters of other students in the class and decide which three you will choose.
2 Discuss and explain the reasons for your choices with the whole class. How many letters are there that you all agree should be published? What makes them so good?

Unit 30 Who's Afraid of the Silicon Chip?

A silicon chip is a tiny metalloid element used in calculators, computers, etc. These are some of the things experts say about the effect the silicon chip is going to have on our lives:

> "Essentially we're facing the second industrial revolution. The first attacked power, with steam. The second is attacking information."
> Ian Barron, Head of Inmos, British Micro-Electric Company

> "It's going to happen. To refuse it would be like a country deciding it's not going to have cars. There's no place to hide."
> Professor John Ashworth, Chief Scientific Advisor, UK Central Policy Review Staff ('Think Tank')

> "It is doubtful whether the public at large has any idea of the revolution in communications which will result from developments in progress."
> Carter Committee Report on the Post Office in Britain

(Quotations from *Observer Magazine*, 18 November 1979.)

Ⓚ **A1** Discuss with the rest of the class how much you know about the silicon chip. Then read the passage below and answer the questions that follow.

Para 1 The one thing that's going to get talked about non-stop throughout the 1980s is about as big as this ▮▮▮▮ .

Para 2 For the electro-technologically minded, it's a miracle of micro-processing wizardry with the mind-boggling potential to revolutionise the whole of life. For the uninitiated, it's a source of bafflement, unease, and a vaguely sci-fi fascination. It represents *the* major challenge of this century's last twenty years, so all the expert futurologists claim, yet sounds to most of us like some new-fangled substitute for fried potato.

Para 3 It's the silicon chip.

Para 4 Not surprisingly, most non-scientists find that the effort of trying to grasp what a silicon chip *is* turns out to be just as bewildering as the struggle to comprehend what a silicon chip *does*.

Para 5 Thirty years ago, the world's first electronic digital computer weighed about thirty tons and filled a room. Today's silicon chip equivalent weighs a fraction of a gramme and would disappear on your fingernail.

Para 6 Once designed, a silicon chip can be ludicrously cheap to manufacture in bulk. That is why everyone can now buy for

115

peanuts such sophisticated gadgetry as pocket calculators or complex TV games. Desk-top computers will soon be as familiar as desk-top typewriters— or electronic word-processors as *they* are all about to become in the chip revolution.

Para 7 Not only is the silicon chip small and ever more inexpensive, it is also reliable and immensely versatile. Already the world market is estimated at £3 billion a year. By the mid-1980s, one chip-maker predicts, every person in the world may need to own at least one microprocessing toy just to find an outlet for the industry's burgeoning supply.

Para 8 Such talk is typical of the increasingly extravagant claims being made on behalf of the silicon chip. It has been called the most significant invention since the wheel. A single chip can far outstrip the mathematical speed and capacity of any man. Multi-chip computers can perform a million error-free calculations in the time it takes to blink and they're getting faster all the time. All that is holding them back is the speed at which data can be programmed in, or applications for them found.

Para 9 More and more small firms will take advantage of small, purpose-programmed computers to keep the books. Instrumentation on cars will get neater and more comprehensive. Telephones will have increased international capability, telephone and television-linked information systems will be more comprehensive and more widespread. Cameras will get smaller

and more automated, fun toys like talking calculators and programmable video gadgets will fight for the home entertainment market. Money will continue to give way to computerised accounting and debiting systems, all kinds of security systems will be rapidly advanced. Shops will keep track of their stock with micro-processing systems, all kind of traffic control will become more efficient, less energy will be wasted by better power systems.

Para 10 The 1980s, in short, will certainly see a gathering pace in the applied use of silicon chips but there is not the remotest chance that application will keep pace with theoretical development. The long-term effects of the micro-processing revolution are incalculable—even for a silicon chip.

Para 11 The most talked-about social implication is, of course, the effect of ever more sophisticated automation on employment. Here, too, there has been a marked tendency to take off into scaremongering with exaggerated claims that silicon chips will cause overnight disruption, making millions redundant. A study by the UK Central Policy Review Staff is characteristically sober: "Reports suggesting large-scale loss of jobs from micro-electronic applications overestimate the speed at which these applications could be introduced and underestimate the new markets created in the process."

(i) What are the different interpretations of the silicon chip according to:

		Interpretations
a	The electro-technologically minded	revolutionise the whole of life
b	The uninitiated (*ie.* those who don't know about it)	
c	Futurologists	
d	Most of us	

(ii) Compare the weight and size of the world's first computer and a silicon chip computer of today:

	Weight	Size
First Computer		
Silicon Chip Computer		

(iii) Explain why pocket calculators, etc. are so relatively cheap nowadays:
_____

(iv) What will 'desk-top typewriters' become? _____
_____

(v) What does the chip-maker's prediction suggest about the micro-processing industry? _____
_____

(vi) What justification is there for referring to the chip as 'the most significant invention since the wheel'? _____
_____
_____

(vii) What applications of the chip are likely to be seen in the following?

a small firms	
b car instruments	
c cameras	
d money	
e energy	

(*viii*) What is the main social implication of the chip? _____

(*ix*) Two contrasting opinions on this are quoted, one 'exaggerated', the other 'sober':

'exaggerated': _____

'sober': _____

2 Compare and check your answers with your partner.

Ⓚ **B Vocabulary**

1 Find words or phrases in the passage that have a similar meaning to the following:

(*i*) mystery *(para 2)* _____

(*ii*) growing, increasing *(para 7)* _____

(*iii*) do much better than *(para 8)* _____

(*iv*) including more *(para 9)* _____

(*v*) be replaced by *(para 9)* _____

2 Work out the meaning of the following from the context in which they are used:

(*i*) mind-boggling *(para 2)* _____

(*ii*) for peanuts *(para 6)* _____

(*iii*) marked *(para 11)* _____

(*iv*) overnight *(para 11)* _____

Ⓣ Ⓚ **C1** You are now going to listen to an interview in which a technological expert discusses some future uses of the silicon chip, particularly in relation to the TV set. Read through the questions and answer them as you listen to the tape.

(*i*) List three of the standard facilities a TV set already has or will have in the near future:

(*a*) _____

(*b*) _____

(*c*) _____

(*ii*) What does a keyboard look like? _____

(*iii*) What new system will make shopping easier? _____

(*iv*) Note down two uses of the keyboard for convenience and entertainment purposes:

(*a*) _____

(*b*) _____

(*v*) Give two examples of people who will benefit from having a TV with a keyboard in their home:

(*a*) _____

(*b*) _____

(*vi*) In addition to video-cassette courses how will the TV help educationally?

_____

(*vii*) Explain one function of the printer. _____

_____

2 Compare and check your answers with your partner. If necessary listen to the tape again.

3 Do you find any of the points mentioned in any way surprising? Can you predict any other uses that the TV set might have?

D *Revolution in the Streets*

1 On the next page is an ordinary High Street before and after the conquest of Britain by the silicon chip. The chip — a tiny tooth-sized fragment of porcelain containing an astonishing quarter of a million transistors — is expected to induce a technological and social upheaval as profound, and painful, as that forced on our ancestors by the Industrial Revolution. The replacement of people by machines is likely to cause widespread unemployment. Our lives will change beyond recognition. And our towns and cities will wear a new and disturbing face. That is one set of arguments, but they are balanced by the claim that, after the initial hardship, we all stand to gain immense benefits.

Work in groups of 3–4. Look at 'Today's Town' and the descriptions of the various activities. With the drawings of 'Tomorrow's Town' to guide you, discuss what you think will happen after the silicon chip revolution. Make a list of your predictions.

2 Discuss your ideas with the rest of the class. How far do you agree?

E Writing

Imagine you are living in the year 2000 — in the post-silicon chip revolution. Write a dialogue between yourself and a child in which you explain how things used to work in the old days of the 1980s compared with nowadays.

Revolution in the Streets

A busy period at the store

Supermarket customers pay the check-out girls

The High Street garage open for business

Pupils and teachers work together

Based on *Observer Magazine*, 18 November 1979.

Oral Functions Bank Grid

#	Function	Unit 1 First Impressions	2 Body Shapes and Behaviour	3 A Friend of a Friend	4 Posture	5 Faces	6 Elemental Truths	7 Doodling	8 Making New Friends	9 Give Us Our Daily Drugs	10 Sharing a Home	11 Housing	12 Your Neighbourhood
1	Asking for and Giving Opinions	X	X	X	X	X	X	X	X	X	X	X	X
2	Explaining and Justifying	X	X	X	X	X	X	X	X	X	X	X	X
3	Asking for and Giving Clarification	X	X	X	X	X	X	X	X	X	X	X	X
4	Expressing Agreement and Disagreement	X	X	X	X	X	X	X	X	X	X	X	X
5	Interrupting	X	X	X	X	X	X	X	X	X	X	X	X
6	Describing People	X			X	X	X	X					
7	Introducing Oneself and Giving Personal Information			X					X				
8	Talking about Likes and Interests								X		X		
9	Expressing Preferences		X						X			X	
10	Making Complaints												
11	Giving Warnings												
12	Asking for and Giving Advice												
13	Asking for More Detailed Information									X			
14	Making and Responding to Suggestions												
15	Making Plans and Proposals												X
16	Talking in Favour of or Against a Proposal												X
17	Making Predictions					X			X				
18	Expressing Degrees of Certainty and Uncertainty							X	X				
19	Making Comparisons											X	
20	Making Generalisations												

	Travel to Work (13)	Teenagers' Leisure and Pleasure (14)	How Much Do You Know about Whales? (15)	What the Papers Said (16)	A Foreign Correspondent (17)	The Soap Opera (18)	Children and Television (19)	The Language of Advertising (20)	Consumer Discrimination (21)	A Change Is as Good as a Rest (22)	Is Being Single Still out of Line? (23)	Living Collectively (24)	Getting Away from It All (25)	The Pneu Wave (26)	Vegetarianism (27)	Schools with a Difference (28)	Super Race? (29)	Who's Afraid of the Silicon Chip? (30)
1	X	X	X	X	X	X	X	X	X	X	X	X	X	X	X	X	X	X
2	X	X	X	X	X	X	X	X	X	X	X	X	X	X	X	X	X	X
3	X	X	X	X	X	X	X	X	X	X	X	X	X	X	X	X	X	X
4	X	X	X	X	X	X	X	X	X	X	X	X	X	X	X	X	X	X
5	X	X	X	X	X	X	X	X	X	X	X	X	X	X	X	X	X	X
6																		
7					X													
8																		
9									X									
10								X			X							
11									X									
12													X					
13	X				X													
14		X	X		X		X				X	X			X			
15														X				
16	X					X								X				
17																		X
18																X		X
19	X		X	X										X				
20	X	X																

Oral Functions Bank

F = Formal
Inf = Informal

1 Asking for and Giving Opinions

(i) Asking for Opinions

F

I was wondering where you stood on the question of X?

What's your position on X?

What's your opinion of X?

What do you think of X?

How do you feel about X?

What do you reckon about X?

What about X?

Inf

(ii) Giving Opinions

F

It would seem to me that

As far as I'm able to judge,

As far as I'm concerned,

From my point of view, I think

In my opinion

Personally, I think

As I see it

Frankly, I think

I reckon

+ SENTENCE

Inf

I Make the following into questions and answers about **opinions** using the language in the boxes above.

   Example:
   (a) What/ think/ Dylan's latest record?
   (b) Personally . . . . awful.

   (a) What do you think of Dylan's latest record?
   (b) Personally, I think it's awful.

1(a) What/ position/ going on strike for more pay?
 (b) As far . . . . judge, it won't help matters.
2(a) How/ feel/ young children smoking?
 (b) In . . . . , it shouldn't be allowed.
3(a) What/ opinion/ the Prime Minister?
 (b) As . . . ., he's doing a good job.
4(a) I/ wondering/ you stood/ question/ the Council's proposal to ban cars from the City Centre?
 (b) From . . . . it will make the town a much better place to live in.
5(a) What/ reckon/ the idea of going to Brazil for our holidays?
 (b) Personally, ... that sounds a great idea!

II Use appropriate language from the boxes above to **ask for and give opinions** in the following situations.

   Example:
   Two friends — John's new haircut.

   What do you think of John's new haircut?
   Frankly, I don't think it suits him at all.

1 Employee to boss — workers' decision to go on strike.
2 Brother to sister — new girlfriend.
3 Member of audience to speaker — the government's new agricultural policy.
4 Two new acquaintances — the bomb that went off in London last night.
5 Two work colleagues — management's decision to close the work canteen.

2 Explaining and Justifying

F

The (main) $\begin{Bmatrix} \text{aim} \\ \text{reason} \\ \text{motive etc.} \end{Bmatrix} \begin{Bmatrix} \text{for} \\ \text{behind} \end{Bmatrix}$ DOING . . . $\begin{Bmatrix} \text{is so that X . . .} \\ \text{is to . . .} \end{Bmatrix}$

Only by DOING . . . $\begin{Bmatrix} \text{can} \\ \text{will} \end{Bmatrix}$ X DO . . .

Taking into account factors like X, then + SENTENCE
You've got to take X into consideration.

The $\begin{Bmatrix} \text{main} \\ \text{most important} \end{Bmatrix}$ point seems to me that + SENTENCE

It seems to me $\begin{Bmatrix} \text{evident} \\ \text{obvious} \end{Bmatrix}$ that + SENTENCE

It may $\begin{Bmatrix} \text{seem} \\ \text{sound etc.} \end{Bmatrix} \begin{Bmatrix} \text{unlikely} \\ \text{impractical etc.} \end{Bmatrix}$, but + SENTENCE

Given the circumstances,
All things considered, $\Big\}$ I think + SENTENCE
In view of X,

On the one hand . . . but on the other hand . . .

SENTENCE + because $\begin{Bmatrix} \text{I'm convinced that} \\ \text{I consider that} \\ \text{I'm sure that} \end{Bmatrix}$ + SENTENCE

It's important to $\begin{Bmatrix} \text{keep X in mind.} \\ \text{remember X.} \end{Bmatrix}$

$\begin{Bmatrix} \text{Think of} \\ \text{Look at} \end{Bmatrix}$ X this way: + SENTENCE

Inf

I Make the following into statements **explaining and justifying** using the language from the box above.

Example:
It/ obvious/ a campaign like ours will be successful.

It seems to me obvious that a campaign like ours will be successful.

1 The main aim/ his moving to the country/ to avoid the noise and pollution of big cities.
2 On/ hand, riding a bicycle is pleasant but on/ hand it can be quite dangerous.
3 The/ important/ seems/ me/ unless we do something now people will starve in the future.
4 It may/ unrealistic/ I'm sure the plan will work.
5 All/ considered,/ she must be a pleasant person to know.

126

II Use appropriate language from the box above to make statements **explaining and justifying** in the following situations:

Example:

Talking to friends — You think it would be a good idea to share a flat together but your friends are not so sure.

It may sound impractical, but it'll be much cheaper if we share a flat, etc.

1 Talking to a group of fellow students — You are discussing the possibility of a Third World War. Your view is that it is very unlikely to happen.
2 Talking at a business meeting — Your colleagues want to organise a special advertising campaign for your new brand of soap powder *Wonderwash*. You think the campaign will be expensive and won't increase sales.
3 Talking at a meeting of residents who live in your area — You are discussing how to prevent the proposed building of a huge new office block which will change the whole character of the area. You are in favour of a very public campaign rather than writing individual letters to the Council in the hope that the proposal will be rejected.
4 Talking to a friend — You have decided to take up the offer of a two-year job doing research into animal behaviour on a remote island in the Pacific. You feel that it is a once-in-a-lifetime opportunity and will also help your career.
5 Talking to members of your class about why you are learning English.

3 Asking for and Giving Clarification

(i) Asking for Clarification

F

I'm afraid I'm not quite clear what you mean by X.

I'm sorry, I don't understand what you mean by X.

I'm sorry, but could you explain what you mean by X?

What (exactly) do you mean by X?

What (exactly) are you trying to say?

What (exactly) are you getting at?

Inf

(ii) Giving Clarification

F

Well, the point I'm trying to make is that...

Well, what I'm trying to say is that...

What I mean is that...   + SENTENCE

All I'm trying to say is that...

Well, what I'm getting at is that...

Inf

127

I Make the following into questions and statements **asking for and giving clarification** using the language in the boxes above.

> *Example:*
> *(a)* I/ afraid/ not/ clear/ mean/ saying that.
> *(b)* Well,/ I mean/ we should all help pay for it.
>
> *(a)* *I'm afraid I'm not quite clear what you mean by saying that.*
> *(b)* *Well, what I mean is that we should all help pay for it.*

1*(a)* Sorry,/ I/ not understand/ you mean/ saying the plans should wait till next year.
 (b) Well,/ point/ I/ make/ if we wait, we'll have more chance of success.
2*(a)* I don't understand your argument. What/ you/ at?
 (b) All/ trying/ say/ it's not just a question of intelligence.
3*(a)* I/ sorry,/ could/ explain/ mean/ their love of revenge.
 (b) Well, what/ trying/ say/ they will always fight back.
4*(a)* I/ afraid/ not clear/ mean/ saying you're disappointed with my work.
 (b) Well, what/ trying/ say/ I think you could have done a much better job.
5*(a)* You say that I'm a sociable outgoing sort of person. What/ mean?
 (b) What/ mean/ you enjoy other people's company, going to parties, etc.

II Use appropriate language from the boxes above to **ask for and give clarification** in the following situations. A should express an opinion and B should ask for clarification in each situation. A should give any clarification he thinks appropriate.

> *Example:*
> A: *I think some advertisements deliberately aim to deceive people.*
> B: *What exactly do you mean?*
> A: *Well, they try and persuade us that life will be much better if only we buy a certain product.*

1 A: Boss — "I think hard work should always be rewarded."
 B: Employee
2 A: Colleague — "Money isn't the only important thing about our job."
 B: Colleague
3 A: Friend — "I think marriage is old-fashioned."
 B: Friend
4 A: Cousin — "Our annual family reunions are always surprising in some way."
 B: Cousin
5 A. Politician — "People are simply not aware of the terrible effects a nuclear bomb could have."
 B: Interviewer

4 Expressing Agreement and Disagreement

(i) Expressing Agreement

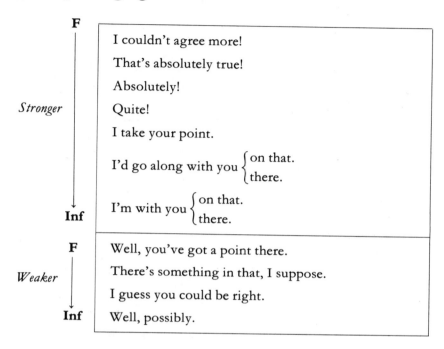

Stronger (F → Inf)	I couldn't agree more!
	That's absolutely true!
	Absolutely!
	Quite!
	I take your point.
	I'd go along with you { on that. / there.
	I'm with you { on that. / there.
Weaker (F → Inf)	Well, you've got a point there.
	There's something in that, I suppose.
	I guess you could be right.
	Well, possibly.

(ii) Expressing Disagreement

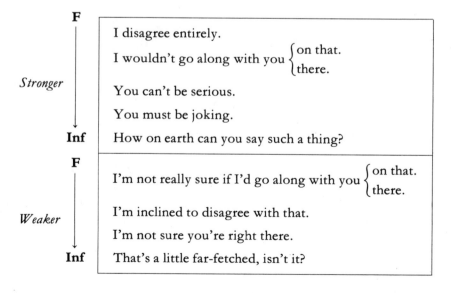

Stronger (F → Inf)	I disagree entirely.
	I wouldn't go along with you { on that. / there.
	You can't be serious.
	You must be joking.
	How on earth can you say such a thing?
Weaker (F → Inf)	I'm not really sure if I'd go along with you { on that. / there.
	I'm inclined to disagree with that.
	I'm not sure you're right there.
	That's a little far-fetched, isn't it?

I Make the following into statements of **agreement and disagreement** using the language in the boxes above.

Example:
(Agree)   I/ not/ more.
(Disagree)   You/ joking.

There's nothing like watching a good football match on TV.
I couldn't agree with you more.
You must be joking.

1 By the year 2000 computer learning in schools will be quite normal.
    There/ something/ suppose.
    I/ not/ go along/ you there.
2 Changes in fashion are just a way of making people spend more money.
    I/ your point.
    I/ inclined to/ with that.
3 Smoking should be banned in all public places.
    I/ go along/ you on that.
    How/ earth/ say/ thing?
4 The Queen is important for tourism in Britain.
    Well,/ you/ point there.
    I/ not sure/ right there.
5 People in affluent societies eat too much.
    That/ absolutely true!
    That/ little far-fetched, isn't it?

II   Use appropriate language from the boxes above to **agree or disagree** in the following situations. Make it clear whether you completely or partially agree.
    NB. You may find it useful to use weaker forms if you want to be sure of being polite.

Example:
Your boss — "People don't work as hard nowadays as they used to."

You — "I'm not sure you're right there."

1 A friend — "I think men with long hair look awful."
2 An elderly relation — "Young people have a really good life these days."
3 A person you have just met — "Very intelligent children should be educated in separate schools."
4 Your sister or brother — "Most pop-singers are also very good-looking."
5 A work colleague — "I think we should ask for a 50% pay rise."

5 Interrupting

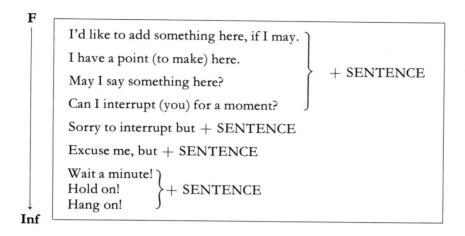

I Make the following into statements **interrupting** another speaker; use the language in the box above.

Example:
Sorry/ interrupt,/ haven't you forgotten Jane?

Sorry to interrupt, but haven't you forgotten Jane?

1 I/ add/ here/ may. There are far more cars on the roads now than 10 years ago.
2 I/ point/ make. If we sell the company now, we may not get such a good price.
3 Sorry/ interrupt,/ I don't think your plan will work.
4 Can I/ you/ moment? Have you thought of going there by train?
5 May/ say/ here? I don't think you've considered the cost of such a campaign.

II Use appropriate language from the box above to **interrupt** in the following situations. A should start talking and B should interrupt in each situation.

Example:
A: Friend — talking about recent exam.
B: Friend.

A: That exam we had last week was awful. I could hardly do . . .
B: Hang on! It wasn't as bad as that . . . etc.

1 A: Host/hostess — talking about rising prices.
　B: Guest.
2 A: Famous person — talking about career.
　B: Journalist.
3 A: Work colleague — talking about asking for a pay rise.
　B: Work colleague.
4 A: Friend — talking about holiday plans.
　B: Friend.

5 A: Interviewer — talking about the post that is vacant.
  B: Job applicant.

6 Describing People

(i) Physical features

> What's he/she like?
>
> What does he/she look like?
> -
> He/ She's X
>
> He/ She's got X

(ii) Personality

> What $\begin{Bmatrix} \text{type} \\ \text{sort} \\ \text{kind} \end{Bmatrix}$ of person is he/she?
>
> What do you make of him/her?
>
> What's he/she like?
> -
> He/she comes across as (being) X
>
> He/she gives the impression of being X
>
> It seems (to me) as if he/she's X
>
> He/she's X
>
> He/she $\begin{Bmatrix} \text{looks} \\ \text{seems} \end{Bmatrix}$ X

I Make the following into questions and answers about **describing people** using the language in the boxes above.

> *Example:*
> What/ person/ he?
> He/ across/ very pleasant.
>
> *What kind of person is he?*
> *He comes across as (being) very pleasant.*

1 What/ she like?
  She/ slim and/ long, fair hair.
2 What/ make/ her?
  She gives/ impression/ being/ difficult to work with.
3 What/ person/ he?
  It/ me as/ very honest and reliable.

132

4 What/ make/ him?

He/ across/ a very confident person.

5 What/ person/ she?

It/ as if/ rather shy.

II Use appropriate language from the boxes above to ask questions and **describe people** in the following situations.

Example:

two friends ————————→ new boss.

A: *What does your new boss look like?*

B: *Well, he's short and quite fat, but he's got a pleasant face.*

A: *What kind of person is he?*

B: *He gives me the impression of being a good person to work for. etc.*

1 Sister to brother ————————→ new girlfriend.

2 Student to student ————————→ new teacher.

3 Two members of the same family ————————→ cousin (who only one of you knows).

4 Two work colleagues ————————→ new employee.

5 Two friends ————————→ famous person (who one of you has just met).

7 Introducing Oneself and Giving Personal Information

F

$\begin{Bmatrix} \text{Allow me to} \\ \text{I'd like to} \end{Bmatrix}$ introduce myself. My name's X. I'm + INFORMATION

eg. I'm from X

I work in X

I live in X etc

May I introduce myself? My name's X. I'm + INFORMATION.

How do you do? My name's X. I'm + INFORMATION.

$\begin{Bmatrix} \text{Hello!} \\ \text{Hi!} \end{Bmatrix}$ I'm X. I'm + INFORMATION.

Inf

Responses

F

Pleased to meet you.

How do you do?

Hello!

Hi!

Inf

133

I Make the following into statements **introducing oneself and giving personal information** using the language in the boxes above.

Example:
Hi! I/ John. I/ student/ this school too.

Hi! I'm John. I'm a student at this school too.

1 Allow/ myself./ Name/ Derek Jones. I/ London and/ TV interviewer.
2 How/ do?/ Name/ Sandra West. I/ from the US and/ here/ holiday.
3 I/ like/ myself./ Name/ Mr Bond and/ from Sydney, Australia.
4 May I/ myself?/ Name/ Joan Brown and/ just started work in the office below.
5 Hello! I/ Terry. I think/ seen you/ this bar before.

II Use appropriate language from the boxes above to **introduce yourself** to each of the people below and suggest an appropriate response.

Example:
A close friend of your sister

— *Hello! I'm X . . . I'm Jane's sister.*
— *Hello!*

1 A new colleague who has just started working with you.
2 A speaker who has just given a talk you enjoyed very much.
3 A small group of people at a friend's party.
4 A famous person you are going to interview for a TV programme.
5 A business man you are going to negotiate a deal with.

8   Talking About Likes and Interests

(i) F

I wonder if you're (at all) interested in $\begin{cases} \text{X?} \\ \text{DOING} \ldots \text{?} \end{cases}$

Are you interested in $\begin{cases} \text{X?} \\ \text{DOING} \ldots \text{?} \end{cases}$

Do you (happen to) like $\begin{cases} \text{X?} \\ \text{DOING} \ldots \text{?} \end{cases}$

Are you into $\begin{cases} \text{X?} \\ \text{DOING} \ldots \text{?} \end{cases}$

Inf

(ii) F

$$I'm \begin{Bmatrix} very \\ quite \end{Bmatrix} interested\ in \begin{Bmatrix} X \\ DOING\ldots \end{Bmatrix}$$

$$I'm \begin{Bmatrix} very \\ quite \end{Bmatrix} keen\ on \begin{Bmatrix} X \\ DOING\ldots \end{Bmatrix}$$

$$I\ (really)\ like \begin{Bmatrix} X \\ DOING\ldots \end{Bmatrix} (very\ much).$$

Inf

$$I'm\ really\ into \begin{Bmatrix} X \\ DOING\ldots \end{Bmatrix}$$

(iii) F

$$I\ don't\ find \begin{Bmatrix} X \\ DOING\ldots \end{Bmatrix} particularly \begin{Bmatrix} enjoyable \\ good \\ interesting. \end{Bmatrix}$$

$$I'm\ not \begin{Bmatrix} over- \\ particularly \end{Bmatrix} keen\ on \begin{Bmatrix} X \\ DOING\ldots \end{Bmatrix}$$

$$I\ don't\ (really)\ like \begin{Bmatrix} X \\ DOING\ldots \end{Bmatrix} (very\ much).$$

Inf

$$I'm\ not\ really\ into \begin{Bmatrix} X \\ DOING\ldots \end{Bmatrix}$$

Ia   Make the following into questions about other people's **likes and interests** using the language in the boxes above.

Example:
Do/ like football?

Do you like football?

1 Are/ interested/ current affairs?
2 Do/ happen/ like jazz music?
3 Are/ into watching TV a lot?
4 I wonder/ you/ at all interested/ international politics?
5 Are/ interested/ the theatre?

b   Make the following into statements about **likes and interests** using the language in the boxes above.

1 I/ not find eating/ restaurants/ enjoyable.
2 I/ keen/ keeping fit.
3 I/ into learning languages.
4 I/ not over-keen/ playing sport.
5 I/ interested/ travelling to new places.

II   Use appropriate language from the boxes above to ask and answer people's **likes and interests** in the following situations:

135

Example:
Two friends at a party —————— discos.

(a) *Are you into discos?*
(b) *No, I'm not particularly keen on them.*

1 Two new acquaintances at a party —————— the theatre.
2 A young member of the family to an elderly relation —————— the Sunday newspapers.
3 An employee to his/her boss —————— watching sports on TV.
4 Two good friends —————— the latest fashion.
5 Two work colleagues —————— going to pubs.

9 Expressing Preferences

F

I tend to favour $\left\{ \begin{array}{l} X \\ DOING\ldots \end{array} \right\}$ as opposed to $\left\{ \begin{array}{l} X \\ DOING\ldots \end{array} \right.$

I tend to prefer $\left\{ \begin{array}{l} X \\ DOING\ldots \end{array} \right\}$ to $\left\{ \begin{array}{l} X \\ DOING\ldots \end{array} \right.$

I tend to be (rather) more interested in $\left\{ \begin{array}{l} X \\ DOING\ldots \end{array} \right\}$ than $\left\{ \begin{array}{l} X \\ DOING\ldots \end{array} \right.$

I'm (rather) more interested in $\left\{ \begin{array}{l} X \\ DOING\ldots \end{array} \right\}$ than $\left\{ \begin{array}{l} X \\ DOING\ldots \end{array} \right.$

I much prefer $\left\{ \begin{array}{l} X \\ DOING\ldots \end{array} \right\}$ to $\left\{ \begin{array}{l} X \\ DOING\ldots \end{array} \right.$

$\left. \begin{array}{l} X \\ DOING\ldots \end{array} \right\}$ appeals to me (far) more than $\left\{ \begin{array}{l} X \\ DOING\ldots \end{array} \right.$

I like $\left\{ \begin{array}{l} X \\ DOING\ldots \end{array} \right\}$ better than $\left\{ \begin{array}{l} X \\ DOING\ldots \end{array} \right.$

Inf

I Make the following into statements about **preferences** using the language in the box above.

Example:
I tend/ favour the proposal put forward at last week's meeting.

I tend to favour the proposal put forward at last week's meeting.

1 I tend/ rather more interested/ going/ classical music concerts.
2 Having a seaside holiday/ me more/ doing winter sports.
3 I /swimming better/ playing football.
4 I/ more interested/ living/ countryside than/ smart flat in town.
5 I tend/ prefer Chinese cooking/ Indian cooking.

II Look at the following and use appropriate language from the box above to make statements about your **preferences**:

Example:
Wine/beer

I prefer wine to beer.
Wine appeals to me more than beer.
etc.

1 Going to the cinema/ going to the theatre.
2 Italian food/ Chinese food.
3 Getting up early/ getting up late.
4 Lively place with lots of night life/ quiet place with very few other people.
5 Reading newspapers/ watching the news on TV.

10 Making Complaints

F

I'd like to $\begin{Bmatrix} \text{make a complaint} \\ \text{complain} \end{Bmatrix}$ about X.

I've got a complaint (to make) about X.

I'm not prepared to $\begin{Bmatrix} \text{tolerate} \\ \text{put up with} \end{Bmatrix}$ X any longer.

I'm rather $\begin{Bmatrix} \text{annoyed} \\ \text{upset} \\ \text{disturbed etc.} \end{Bmatrix}$ about X.

I've had enough of X DOING . . .

I'm fed up with X DOING . . .

It's about time X DID . . .

X is driving me $\begin{cases} \text{mad.} \\ \text{round the bend.} \end{cases}$

Inf

I Make the following into statements of **complaint** using the language in the box above.

Example:
I/ enough/ Jane wasting my time.

I've had enough of Jane wasting my time.

1 I/ like/ a complaint/ the television set I bought here yesterday.
2 It/ time/ John offered to help with the washing-up.
3 I/ prepared/ tolerate this rude behaviour/ longer.
4 I/ complaint/ make/ the loud music you play at night.
5 I/ enough/ buying goods which are nothing like the advertisements claim.

137

II Use appropriate language from the box to **make complaints** in the following situations.

> *Example:*
> Your younger brother is always playing pop records very loudly.
>
> *I'm fed up with listening to your records every minute of the day.*
> *They're driving me mad.*
> *etc.*

1 Your new neighbours' son is learning how to play the saxophone and practises for three hours every evening.

2 You are in a smart restaurant and the food you ordered half an hour ago has just been served. You discover that it is cold and not properly cooked.

3 Yesterday evening at 6.30 pm a violent thriller film was shown on TV. Your two young children watched it and were very upset and frightened. You decide to phone the director of the TV company.

4 You share a flat with some fellow students. One of them never helps in the house at all and expects everything to be done for him/her by the rest of you. You decide to speak to him/her.

5 Last week you booked your holiday flight to a Caribbean Island. At the time the cost of the flight seemed remarkably low. This morning you received a letter from the travel agent informing you that the flight is cancelled and your money non-refundable. You decide to go and see the travel agent.

11   Giving Warnings

F

If you take my advice, you won't DO . . .

Let me warn you $\begin{cases} \text{about} \\ \text{off} \\ \text{against} \end{cases}$ $\begin{array}{l} \text{DOING} \ldots \\ \text{X} \end{array}$

One thing I wouldn't do is DO . . .

If my experience is anything to go by, you shouldn't DO . . .

You'd do best not to DO . . .

Whatever you do, don't DO . . .

Beware of $\begin{cases} \text{DOING} \ldots \\ \text{X} \end{cases}$

Watch out for X

Don't DO . . .

Inf

I Make the following into statements **giving warnings,** using the language in the box above.

Example:
You/ best not/ go there.

You'd do best not to go there.

1 If/ take/ advice,/ not give that building firm a contract for the job.
2 Whatever/ do,/ not eat in that fish restaurant.
3 Beware/ swimming in the sea near those rocks.
4 Let/ warn you/ buying things in that shop.
5 If/ experience/ go by, you/ not try to change the way they run the office.

II Use the appropriate language from the box above to **give warnings** in the following situations.

Example:
Warn a friend about a new disco that you know is expensive and plays bad music.

Whatever you do, don't go to that disco ... etc.

1 Warn your boss about employing someone who you know to be dishonest and unreliable.
2 Warn a group of foreign visitors to your country about things, *eg.* prices, customs, etc. which you think they should be aware of.
3 Warn a friend who has decided to hitch-hike around the world on his/her own about some of the dangers involved.
4 Warn your parents about visiting a place that you went to last year and did not like.
5 Warn an acquaintance who has had too much to drink at a party and yet insists on driving home.

12 Asking for and Giving Advice

(i) Asking for advice

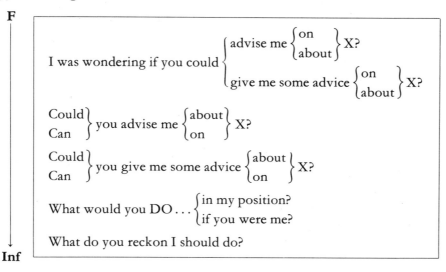

(ii) Giving advice

F

> I think your best course would be to DO...
>
> I'd advise you to DO...
>
> You might (like to) try $\begin{cases} \text{X} \\ \text{DOING} \ldots \end{cases}$
>
> You could consider $\begin{cases} \text{X} \\ \text{DOING} \ldots \end{cases}$
>
> If I were you, I'd DO...
>
> I suggest you DO...
>
> I think you $\begin{cases} \text{should} \\ \text{ought to} \end{cases}$ DO...
>
> I think you'd better DO...
>
> Why don't you DO...?

Inf

I Make the following into statements **asking for and giving advice** using the language in the boxes above.

Example:
(a) Can/ me/ advice/ what to wear to the party?
(b) I suggest/ wear/ long dress.

(a) *Can you give me some advice about what to wear to the party?*
(b) *I suggest you wear a long dress.*

1(a) I/ wondering/ you/ advice/ going to University in England?
(b) I/ your/ course/ be/ find out first which universities offer the subject you want to study.
2(a) Could/ advise/ buying a second-hand car?
(b) Why/ you look at the advertisements in the newspaper?
3(a) I hate my job and I'm thinking of leaving it. What/ reckon/ do?
(b) I think/ better make sure you've got another one to go to first.
4(a) I find it difficult to make friends living in a big city. What/ do if/ me?
(b) I think/ ought/ try and join a social club in the area where you live.
5(a) Can/ give/ advice/ what to say to the children?
(b) I suggest/ tell them it was an accident.

II Use appropriate language from the boxes above to **ask for and give advice** in the following situations.

Example:
A: Someone who owes other people lots of money.
B: A friend.

140

A: What do you reckon I should do about my debts?

B: Well, I think you ought to get a job and start paying back the money you owe.

1 A: Someone who is trying to give up smoking.
  B: A doctor.
2 A: Someone who is worried about doing important exams next week.
  B: A relative.
3 A: Someone who feels life is always 'dull'.
  B: A friend.
4 A: Someone who is visiting your country for the first time and wants to know what to see and do.
  B: Yourself.
5 A: Someone who doesn't know what to do after leaving school.
  B: Careers adviser.

13 Asking for More Detailed Information

F

I wonder if you could explain $\begin{cases} \text{about X} \\ \text{how you DO} \ldots \end{cases}$ in (rather) more detail?

Could I ask you a little more about $\begin{cases} \text{X} \\ \text{how you DO} \ldots \end{cases}$

I'm afraid I'm not quite clear $\begin{cases} \text{about X} \\ \text{how you DO} \ldots \end{cases}$

I'm interested in knowing more about X.

How (exactly) do you DO . . .?

Could you fill me in a bit on $\begin{cases} \text{X?} \\ \text{how you DO} \ldots ? \end{cases}$

Can you put me in the picture about X?

Inf

I Make the following into questions or statements **asking for more detailed information** using the language in the box above.

Example:
Could/ ask/ about your political views?

Could I ask you a bit more about your political views?

1 I/ interested/ knowing/ your country.
2 I/ afraid/ not quite clear/ you pay the rent.
3 Could/ fill/ in/ your career up to now?
4 I wonder/ you/ explain/ your new camera works.
5 Can/ me/ picture/ our new neighbours?

141

II Use appropriate language from the box above to **ask for more detailed information** in the following situations.

> *Example:*
> You are talking to a well-known photographer. Ask for more details about his camera and the techniques he uses.
>
> *Could I ask you a bit more about the photos you take at night? How exactly do you achieve such a remarkable effect?*

1 You are at an interview for a job as assistant to a safari hunter. Ask for more details about the job.
2 You are talking to a fellow student about a mutual friend who suddenly got married last week-end. Ask for more details about how your friend met his/her new wife/husband.
3 You are talking to your boss who has just refused to give you a pay rise. Ask for more detailed reasons.
4 You are at a public lecture on urban pollution but the speaker has only mentioned the effects of noise in very general terms. Ask for more details.
5 You are interviewing a famous person for a TV programme. Ask for more details about his/her career.

14   Making and Responding to Suggestions

(i)   Making Suggestions

F

> If I might make a suggestion, we could DO . . .
>
> I suggest we DO . . .
>
> Wouldn't it be a good idea to DO . . . ?
>
> How does the idea of DOING . . . appeal to you?
>
> We could always DO . . .
>
> Why don't we DO . . . ?
>
> What ⎫
> How ⎭ about DOING . . . ?
>
> I've got a ⎰ great ⎱ idea; we could DO . . .
>   ⎱ good ⎰
>
> Let's DO . . .

Inf

142

(ii) Responding to Suggestions

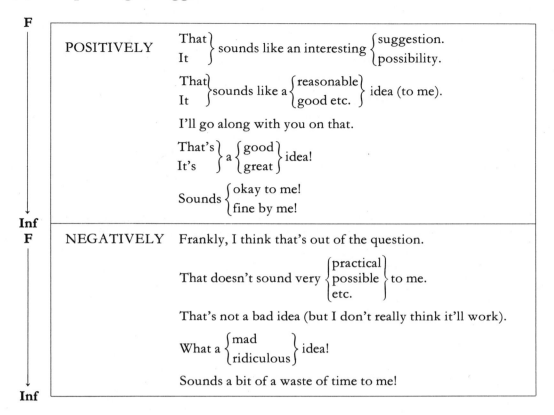

I Make the following into ways of **making and responding to suggestions** using the language in the boxes above.

Example:
(a) How/ idea/ organising/ campaign/ to you?
(b) It/ like/ excellent idea.

(a) *How does the idea of organising a campaign appeal to you?*
(b) *It sounds like an excellent idea.*

1(a) Why/ we try and help her find a job?
 (b) Sounds/ good idea/ me.
2(a) If/ make/ suggestion, we/ redecorate the house completely.
 (b) Frankly, I/ that/ question.
3(a) How/ giving a party to raise some money?
 (b) That/ not sound realistic/ me.
4(a) We/ always move out of the city!
 (b) That/ not/ bad idea.
5(a) How/ idea/ living on a houseboat/ to you?
 (b) What/ ridiculous idea!

II Use appropriate language from the boxes above to **make and respond to suggestions** in the following situations.

Example:
Talking to work colleagues about the present for your boss who is leaving at the end of the week.

— *I suggest we buy him a tie.*
— *That doesn't sound a very sensible idea. He hates wearing ties.*

1 Talking to members of your family about ways to brighten up your living room.
2 Talking to a group of students about how to help a fellow student who has been threatened with expulsion from your college for being found drunk after a party.
3 Talking to friends about a TV play you are planning to write together.
4 Talking to fellow members of a committee which is currently organising a campaign — 'Save paper, protect trees!'
5 Talking to some new acquaintances who are staying in your house about how to spend the day.

15   Making Plans and Proposals

F

I would like to put forward a proposal that + SENTENCE

I would like to propose that + SENTENCE

What I $\begin{Bmatrix} \text{propose} \\ \text{suggest} \end{Bmatrix}$ is $\begin{Bmatrix} \text{to} \\ \text{that} \end{Bmatrix}$ + SENTENCE

My $\begin{Bmatrix} \text{idea} \\ \text{proposal} \end{Bmatrix}$ is $\begin{Bmatrix} \text{to} \\ \text{that} \end{Bmatrix}$ + SENTENCE

There's only one $\begin{Bmatrix} \text{thing to be done.} \\ \text{way to solve the problem.} \end{Bmatrix}$ + SENTENCE

One $\begin{Bmatrix} \text{possibility} \\ \text{way out} \end{Bmatrix}$ would be to + SENTENCE

I've got a $\begin{Bmatrix} \text{great} \\ \text{good} \end{Bmatrix}$ idea! If + SENTENCE

Inf

I   Make the following into statements putting forward **plans and proposals** using the language in the box above.

Example:
What/ propose/ write a letter to the *Times*.

What I propose is to write a letter to the Times.

1 I/ like/ forward/ proposal/ we continue the meeting tomorrow.
2 My idea/ no-one should have to pay to go to work.
3 One/ out/ be/ go camping and not stay in expensive hotels.
4 There/ only/ way/ problem. That is to open a new youth club.
5 I/ great idea! If everybody helps pay for petrol it'll cost much less to get there.

II Use appropriate language from the box above to **make plans and proposals** in the following situations.

Example:
An informal meeting with work colleagues about bad conditions in your office.

My idea is that we should write a letter to the management asking for improvements.

1 A formal business meeting about how to organise a new advertising campaign for your firm's product.
2 Talking with a group of friends about how you can all meet up on holiday this year.
3 A meeting with people, who you don't know very well but who share your ideas, to discuss an anti-pollution campaign you are organising together.
4 A college cultural committee meeting to plan end-of-term entertainments.
5 An informal meeting with neighbours to discuss the problem of a noisy disco which has just opened in your area.

16   Talking in Favour of or Against a Proposal

(i)   In Favour of a Proposal*

I'm completely behind the proposal to DO . . .

I thoroughly approve of $\begin{cases} X \\ DOING \ldots \end{cases}$

I wholeheartedly agree with $\begin{cases} X \\ DOING \ldots \end{cases}$

The proposal to DO . . . has my full $\begin{cases} \text{support.} \\ \text{backing.} \end{cases}$

I'd like to support the proposal to DO . . .

145

(ii) Against a Proposal*

> I see no valid reasons for supporting the proposal to DO...
>
> I am wholly opposed to the proposal to DO...
>
> I am sure it's not $\begin{Bmatrix} \text{feasible} \\ \text{possible} \end{Bmatrix}$ to DO...
>
> I can see many $\begin{Bmatrix} \text{problems} \\ \text{dangers} \end{Bmatrix}$ in (adopting) the proposal to DO...

I   Make the following into statements **talking in favour of or against a proposal** using the language in the boxes.

Example:
I/ behind/ proposal/ ban smoking.

I am completely behind the proposal to ban smoking.

1 The proposal/ support the strike/ full support.
2 I/ wholly opposed/ proposal/ increase the price of public transport.
3 I/ like/ support/ proposal/ ban cars from the centre of town.
4 I/ approve/ children watching as much TV as they like.
5 I/ sure/ not feasible/ stop children from watching TV.

II   Use appropriate language from the boxes above to **talk in favour of or against** the following proposals.

Example:
Pubs should stay open as long as they like.

I can see no valid reasons for supporting this proposal.

1 Children should be made to stay at school until they are 16.
2 Public transport should be free.
3 University students should pay for their education.
4 Prisons should be abolished and some more humane way of treating prisoners be found.
5 Factories causing pollution should be closed down.

---

*NB: The usual context for talking in favour of or against a proposal is assumed to be formal meetings. No indication of formality and informality is given here, since ALL THE EXPRESSIONS ARE FAIRLY FORMAL.

17 Making Predictions

F

He/she / X
- is sure to
- is bound to
- will probably
- is probably going to

DO... / HAPPEN

It's not { out of the question / impossible } that { he/she / X } will { DO... / HAPPEN }

It's (quite) { likely / probable } that { he/she / X } will { DO... / HAPPEN }

He/she / X } may (well) { DO... / HAPPEN }

It's on the cards that { he/she / X } will { DO... / HAPPEN }

Inf

I Make the following into statements about **predictions** using the language in the box above.

Example:
It/ likely/ West Germany/ win the World Cup.

It's quite likely that West Germany will win the World Cup.

1 It/ not out/ question/ he/ arrive tonight.
2 It/ cards/ they/ change their minds.
3 He/ bound/ have a successful career.
4 It/ not impossible/ we/ finish it today.
5 It/ probable/ they/ hold another meeting next week.

II Use the appropriate language from the box above to **make predictions** about the following:

Example: Schools

It's quite likely that schools as we know them today won't exist. Children will probably learn by computer, etc.

1 Nuclear War.
2 Overpopulation and the world shortage of food.
3 Yourself in five years time.
4 The government of your country.
5 The way people will be living in the year 2000.

147

18 Expressing Degrees of Certainty and Uncertainty

CERTAIN	X will undoubtedly happen.	
	X will $\begin{Bmatrix} \text{definitely} \\ \text{certainly} \end{Bmatrix}$ happen.	
	X is $\begin{Bmatrix} \text{bound} \\ \text{sure} \end{Bmatrix}$ to happen.	
ALMOST CERTAIN	It's $\begin{Bmatrix} \text{almost} \\ \text{virtually} \end{Bmatrix}$ certain that + SENTENCE	
	X will almost $\begin{Bmatrix} \text{certainly} \\ \text{definitely} \end{Bmatrix}$ happen.	
	It's very probable that + SENTENCE	
	There's every chance that + SENTENCE	
POSSIBLE	X $\begin{Bmatrix} \text{might well} \\ \text{may well} \\ \text{could well} \end{Bmatrix}$ happen.	
	It's possible that + SENTENCE	
	There's a good chance that + SENTENCE	
UNLIKELY	It is $\begin{Bmatrix} \text{most improbable} \\ \text{very unlikely} \end{Bmatrix}$ that + SENTENCE	
	There's $\begin{Bmatrix} \text{a hundred to one} \\ \text{an outside} \end{Bmatrix}$ chance that + SENTENCE	
IMPOSSIBLE	X $\begin{Bmatrix} \text{definitely} \\ \text{certainly} \end{Bmatrix}$ won't happen.	
	There's no $\begin{Bmatrix} \text{chance} \\ \text{way} \end{Bmatrix}$ that + SENTENCE	

(margin annotations on left: F ... Inf repeated for each box)

I Make the following into statements **expressing degrees of certainty and uncertainty** using the language in the boxes above.

Example:
He/ bound/ find a good job.

He's bound to find a good job.

1 There/ every chance/ she/ recover from the accident.
2 There/ no way/ he/ lend me money.
3 It/ very unlikely/ wealthy people live in houses like that.
4 It/ virtually certain / unemployment will get worse.

148

5 There/ hundred/ chance/ someone who takes strong drugs regularly will give them up.

II   Use appropriate language from the boxes above to make statements **expressing degrees of certainty and uncertainty** about the following.

Example:
The effect of rising prices.

There's every chance that rising prices will lead to an increase in political violence.
etc.

1 The effect of drugs on young people.
2 The influence of astrology on people's personalities.
3 The possibility of creating a World Government.
4 The relation between crime and social background.
5 The influence of advertising on what people buy.

19   Making Comparisons

F

$X \begin{Bmatrix} \text{differs} \\ \text{varies} \end{Bmatrix}$ from Y in that + SENTENCE

The (main) difference between X and Y is that + SENTENCE

One of the differences between X and Y is that + SENTENCE

One of the (main) (dis-)advantages of $\begin{Bmatrix} \text{X} \\ \text{DOING}\ldots \end{Bmatrix}$ is that + SENTENCE

X has an advantage over Y in that + SENTENCE

$X \begin{Bmatrix} \text{is} \\ \text{comes off} \end{Bmatrix}$ better than Y because + SENTENCE

X is more (+ adjective) than Y because + SENTENCE

X is not $\begin{Bmatrix} \text{as} \\ \text{so} \end{Bmatrix}$ (+ adjective) as Y because + SENTENCE

There's no comparison between X and Y. X is + SENTENCE

Inf

I   Make the following into statements of **comparison** using the language in the box above.

Example:
The Times newspaper differs/ the *Sun*/ more serious.

The Times newspaper differs from the Sun in that it is more serious.

1 The main difference/ Chinese food/ Japanese food/ Chinese food/ richer.
2 Jane/ an advantage/ Mary/ she already speaks three languages.
3 Public schools/ off better/ state schools because they have more money.
4 One/ advantages/ travelling by bicycle/ you get some exercise.
5 There/ comparison/ fresh fruit/ tinned fruit. Fresh fruit is far more delicious.

II Use appropriate language from the box above to make statements of **comparison** about the following:

Example:
Home-made cakes/ cakes bought in a shop.

There's no comparison between home-made cakes and cakes bought in a shop. Home-made cakes are far better.
etc.

1 Travelling by train/ travelling by car.
2 Apes/ human beings.
3 Day school/ boarding school.
4 Smoking cigarettes/ drinking alcohol.
5 The different newspapers in your country.

20 Making Generalisations

F

There is a tendency for X (not) to DO . . .

X has a tendency (not) to DO . . .

X is inclined (not) to DO . . .

X tends (not) to DO . . .

$X \begin{Bmatrix} \text{seems} \\ \text{appears} \end{Bmatrix}$ to DO . . .

In the vast majority of cases,
In most cases,
Generally (speaking), $\Big\}$ + SENTENCE
By and large,
On the whole,

Inf

I Make the following into statements about **generalisations** using the language in the box above.

Example:
English people/ tendency/ drink a lot of tea.

English people have a tendency to drink a lot of tea.

1 In/ majority/ cases, historic buildings have been preserved by the Council.
2 Very intelligent children/ inclined/ bored at school.
3 Children always/ to like chocolate and ice-cream.
4 There/ tendency/ people/ come to work by car.
5 Working people/ choose holidays which are different from their daily routine.

II   Use appropriate language from the box above to make **generalisations** about the following:

Example:
People's attitude towards nuclear war.

People tend to think a nuclear war won't really happen.
etc.

1 English people and their way of life.
2 Your own nationality and the way of life in your country.
3 What it's like to be a teenager.
4 The expansion of air travel and its effect on tourism.
5 Politicians.

Gapped Tapescripts

Unit 3   Friend of a Friend

1   *Telephone ringing.*
Cathy: Hello.
Hitchhiker: Oh, er, hello, is, that Cathy O'Brien speaking?
C: Yes.
HH: Er, hello, my name's, er, Terry Jordan. Er, I'm a friend of a friend of yours, er, Bill Evans.
C: Bill Evans?
HH: Yeah, Bill Evans, he's, he's, um, said he knew you very well, er, and, er, *(1)* _____, I think, and um, he told me I should look you up.
C: At university with me? Bill Evans?
HH: Yeah.
C: You don't, you don't, you don't mean Bill Evans who used to drink with my brother, do you?
HH: Well, it could be. He certainly said he knew you very well, er, he's in Australia now.
C: That's right *(yeah, that's right)*, yes, yes, he used to drink with my brother quite a lot. He caused quite a lot of trouble in fact.
HH: Oh, I, er, well, I — he enjoys a good time, I know that I, er, you know, have a drink with him myself on occasion, but he's, he *(2)* _____ quite well in Sydney and, er, he asked me to look you up and give him his best wishes — give you his best wishes.
C: Well, I'm afraid I'm not terribly interested in hearing from or about Bill Evans. As I say, he caused a lot of trouble. It seems absolutely typical of him that he would be so insensitive as to give people's phone numbers. Ah!
HH: I'm, er, he certainly didn't give me that impression and, er, he said that, erm, if I were stuck, you know, er, any time in London, passing through, that, em, you might be able to help me, you know, put me up for a night or two.

C: He never did know *(3)* _____ _____. He just thought everyone lived in the same, same sort of way as he did *(well, I . . .)* well, I'm, I'm, I'm sorry, I mean, you know, it's just, well, in any case, it's impossible *(well)* it really is impossible.
HH: I'm sorry, er, that it's upset you so much, um, perhaps I could just take you out for a drink, or, or something this evening, and, and, er, perhaps we could have, just have a chat anyway *(well)*. It *(4)* _____ somebody in London, I don't really know anybody here.
C: I'm, I'm very sorry but we, we, actually, we haven't got any room at all, um, and er, I just *(5)* _____ particularly want to put up a friend of Bill Evans, even if we had.
HH: I, I have my own sleeping bag. I certainly don't mind floors or anything like that, er, perfectly happy really.
C: Well, I, I, I know my, my husband would be extremely upset. I'm, I'm really amazed, well, I'm not amazed really, but I . . . that *(6)* _____ our number. No, I, I'm very sorry, um, but, er, it's, it's just not on. I'm sorry.
HH: Sorry you feel that way about it and sorry *(7)* _____, um, perhaps we'll meet again. Bye, bye.
C: Bye.

2   *Telephone ringing.*
Norman: Hello. 6264211.
HH: Ah, hello, is, is that Norman Bowes, please?
N: Yes, that's right.
HH: Um, hello, er, you don't know me, my name's Terry Jordan, er, I'm a friend of a friend of yours, a fellow called Bill Evans.

152

N: Bill . . . Bill Evans? Er . . .

HH: Yes, yes, Bill Evans, um, he said he knew you very well.

N: Well, he used to share, I think, he used to share a flat with my brother, but, er, I *(well)* wouldn't say *(8)* _____ _____, actually, but . . .

HH: Um, well, you know, he asked me to send his, er, regards, er, you know he's in, in Australia now.

N: Er, I didn't actually, no.

HH: I've just, er, come from Australia overland and, er, just planning to spend a, a short time in, in the south before I go north to see my folks, and, er, *(yeah)* he thought *(9)* _____ to get in touch with you and, and, er, just pass on his best wishes.

N: Well, er, that's very kind of you, thanks a lot.

HH: Yeah, um, in fact I, I'm, he suggested I might look you up, that, er, *(10)* _____ _____ just to go out and have a drink together or something like that.

N: Erm, well, it's, it's a little bit, to tell you the truth, it's a little bit awkward at the moment, er, you know, my wife's not very well actually, in fact, she's in bed *(oh, I'm)* with flu and, er, you know, we've got a couple of kids who're *(I'm sorry about that)* . . . when were you thinking of?

HH: Well, I thought we might, er, maybe go out this evening. I was planning to spend a, a some time in London and, er, actually Bill suggested that, er you *(11)* _____ a bed for the night.

N: Oh, I see. Erm, could you just hang on a minute?

HH: Sure, yeah.

N: Er, look, erm, George, was it?

HH: Er, no, Terry.

N: Terry, sorry. Erm, I think, I really think it's, it's a bit awkward at the moment, erm, er, *(12)* _____ people you could get in touch with?

HH: It's a bit difficult really. I don't know too many people in London and, erm, you know, I wasn't planning to stay too

long, just, er, long enough to, er, perhaps get my bearings again and before I went back up north to see my folks *(well look)* just be for a night or two.

N: Okay, look, *(13)* _____. Erm, we'll, we'll have a word about it, you know, it's not really very easy at the moment and, you know, perhaps, could you ring me back, say, in about, erm, an hour and a half, something like that?

HH: Sure, sure *(and, er)*. That would be fine.

N: And see what we can fix up.

HH: Okay. Um, I'll ring you back then.

N: Okay then.

HH: Okay.

N: Cheers.

HH: Bye, bye.

3 *Telephone ringing.*

Jan: Hello.

HH: Er, hello. Is, is that Jan Simpson?

J: Yes, it is.

HH: Er, hello. Er, my name's Terry Jordan, er, *(ah, ha)* you don't know me but, but, erm, I'm a friend of a friend of yours, a chap called Bill Evans.

J: Bill Evans! Never! *(yeah, yeah)* How on earth do you know Bill?

HH: Well, I was out, *(14)* _____ _____ in Australia _____ and, er, I met Bill, er, in Sydney and we used to see each other quite a lot, you know *(Good Heavens . . .)* and have a few drinks together.

J: He used to work in the Star and Garter. *(Did he?)* How amazing! And then he went off to Australia *(yeah)*. That must be about three years ago or so.

HH: Yes, yes, oh, he's well settled in now. Um . . .

J: H . . . How's he doing?

HH: Oh, he's doing very well indeed. *(15)* _____ there now, you know, his job's going well *(mm)* and, er, he has a good social life *(mm, mm, mm)*. Anyway, he suggested that, er, as I was going to be in London for a short time that I, I might look you up.

J: Sure, sure, good idea.

HH: Yeah, um, I wonder . . . you know, I don't really know very many people and, em, I'm a bit stuck for somewhere to stay. I, I wondered if, er, *(16)* _____ _____ *(you're . . .)* put me up for a night or two.

J: You're stuck for somewhere to stay. Well, *(yeah)* we've got a spare room here. You, you could, you could come and kip on, kip down here if you like.

HH: That, that would be *(um)* absolutely fantastic if I could . . .

J: It's not much, I must say, I mean, we use it really as a junk room but if you don't mind . . .

HH: Well, that . . . no, that doesn't matter, you know, I, *(17)* _____ out anywhere . . .

J: If you don't mind, sort of, I don't know, I suppose you've got a sleeping bag *(yes, I've got everything I need)* and you could just kip down, well, of course you're very, very, very welcome in-indeed.

HH: Well, that's great. I'll, I'll *(come round)* come round as soon as I can then.

J: Well, yes, have you got my address?

HH: Er, I've got an address, um, would you like to give me your address and I'll just check.

J: Yes, okay, well, it's, it's 31 Ferndene Court, and that's, erm, London W.12.

HH: That's right, that's the address I've got.

J: Okay, and *(18)* _____ from the tube. If you get yourself to Shepherds Bush and then just ask. It's about three minutes' walk.

HH: That's fine. No problem, I've got an 'A to Z' anyway so *(um)* I shouldn't have any trouble.

J: Okay, fine, well see you in, in a, in a short while *(yeah)* we can catch up news on Bill *(fine)* okay.

HH: See you soon. Thanks again.

J: Bye, bye, then.

HH: Bye, bye.

Unit 5 Faces

First Description:

This person doesn't have very striking features and wouldn't particularly stand out in a crowd. The hair is dark, straight and *(1)* _____ and the mouth is small and with thin lips. The nose is fairly small and rounded. The overall look is of a fresh-faced person with probably a rather self-effacing personality — serious and reliable but probably fairly naive.

(2) _____ this person is on the tall side and quite strongly built. As for interests, er, I think this person looks the sort who doesn't seek out other people's company but prefers to be alone — probably likes reading and going for walks.

Second Description:

The second person has dark, lively-looking eyes and fairly dark hair — the complexion, however, is rather fair. The nose is on the small side and somewhat pointed.

This person looks the type who leads an active social life — somebody who likes going to parties, likes fast cars, etc. In my opinion this person is probably a lot of fun to be with — but also probably has many ups and downs — *(3)* _____ a pretty sharp temper.

From the head and shoulders it looks as if this person is rather short — a neat, compact build. Overall I get the impression of an alert, intelligent, good-looking person — *(4)* _____ fools.

Third Description:

Well, the third person has a nice, friendly and confident look — in fact could well be an over-confident sort of person at times, I should think. The eyes are dark and have an attractive sparkle. The nose is not very large but rather broad. The hair is dark and pushed to one side.

(5) _____ a strong personality; jovial and good company. Probably gets on easily and well with the opposite sex. From the head and shoulders I think this person is very likely to be stocky — and probably rather overweight.

(6) _____, em, I would imagine this person very much enjoys eating out in restaurants. Sport also — but as a spectator rather than a player.

Fourth Description:

The fourth person's features suggest a kind and reserved personality — someone who is not especially easy to get to know but who with time would become a very good, reliable friend.

This person has warm, honest-looking eyes, rather thin lips and long, dark, shiny hair — *(7)* _____ quite an attractive, rather angular face. From the facial appearance I would imagine this person to be quite tall and slim — probably even on the skinny side.

I imagine this person has what many people would consider rather serious interests, like opera and gardening. Probably also *(8)* _____.

Unit 11   Housing

1   Well, er, where we live now is, er, is, er, a small flat in a modern apartment block and it's, it's okay but *(1)* _____ really. Ideally, what we need, we think, is one of these big older-style semis, you know, the ones that have those very big rooms. This would give us something *(2)* _____ ever since we got married which is, which is space, both for ourselves and for the children. Apart from the usual sort of living areas, what we really want is a bedroom not only for us but for each child so that they can spread out and create a bit of space for themselves. We'd also love for the first time in our lives to have, er, two bathrooms, one for the children, one for us — there's nothing more frustrating than trying to get into a bathroom first thing in the morning, er, *(3)* _____ of three other ladies. The, um, other things that we would like in a house would be one room where the children could get away from us, because we feel that they need to escape from us occasionally just as we need to escape from them and a playroom where, for them, where they could spread out all their toys and, and er, have their friends and, just generally lead their own lives their way without being bothered by us all the time — and conversely we would like, as parents, er, a study room or a workroom where we could escape from the children every now and then just to get on with the things we particularly wanted to do. We have a lot of hobbies and *(4)* _____ if we could have a house with cellars — and that would be very attractive to us, particularly as as my wife is, er, a keen winemaker. An important thing for us would be a garden for two reasons, really, the first is that, er, we both enjoy gardening, particularly vegetable gardening, and providing our own fresh vegetables during the year, but also, er, to provide some outdoor space for the children where they can again get out and enjoy themselves and romp about. I think that more or less sums up the main things *(5)* _____ in our ideal house.

2   Well, I'm living in this, er, attic at the moment, it's a large, old, Victorian house. It's, it's very nice actually, it's self-contained, you go up this staircase right to the top and it's got, er, a sloping roof and beams and things like that but, er, the, the be . . . the living-room and the kitchen *(6)* _____ so all the cooking smells, you know *(7)* _____ when you have people round. It's got a separate bathroom and a separate bedroom but it's, it's very, very cramped and, er, really *(8)* _____ is to find a small terrace house somewhere, you know, something with three bedrooms, something

155

like that, so that, um, you know, you could have people to stay because the trouble is at the moment I . . . people have to sleep on the floor and really that's not very nice. Um, being a professional person, I, I want to keep a room as a study as well which isn't possible at the moment. I'm not really fussy about a garden or a garage or anything like that, er, just perhaps a little bit of space to sit out in when it's warm. Er, one of the things I, I am looking for is, is a large kitchen actually because I think, er, I'd like to be able to use that as a, as a, dining room and *(9)* _____ one of the other rooms, um, as a study or, or, or an extra bedroom or even a room I could even have someone in, rent a room out to, to somebody and have someone living in with me, I think that would be quite a good idea.

3   At the moment I'm living in a bedsitter in the middle of town. It's rather small and dingy and the furniture's very shabby and there's not much room, there's not much space to cook, I've only got a very small cooker. Where I'd really like to live is in a large open-plan studio-flat on about the third or fourth floor. *(10)* _____ really light and ideally to have french windows on to a veranda which overlooked a park, in the middle of the city because *(11)* _____ in the centre of town. I'd paint the flat all white and have a few big pictures on the wall and lots of plants around the place and I'd have cushions, big cushions on the floor. The kitchen would be small but very compact and I'd have lots of machines, I'd have a dishwasher and a washing machine and a micro-wa-wave oven as well because I don't like cooking very much and *(12)* _____ _____ as convenient as possible. Erm, my bedroom would be fairly large and apart from that the only other room would be the living space which would have french windows on to a veranda overlooking the park. And that would be my ideal place to live.

Unit 14   Teenagers' Leisure and Pleasure

Interviewer: I wonder if you could tell us how teenagers spend their non-working hours, um, for example, is there any truth in the claim that they, they spend a lot of time slumped in front of the television?

Sociologist: Yes, there is and, er, *(1)* _____ _____ by a survey that was carried out in 1974 when 14,000 boys and girls who reached the age of sixteen in that year, ah, were interviewed. Er, the results were published by the way in 1976. Er, as far as TV was concerned, 65% of them said that they often watched television.

Int: Ah ha, and what about, er, reading for pleasure. Is, is, is there any evidence that, er, teenagers no longer do much of this?

Soc: Well, this . . . this *(2)* _____ _____. Um, while it's true that 24% in the survey said they hardly ever, or never, did any reading which wasn't connected with school work, er, 27% claimed that they often did non-school reading, or reading for pleasure.

Int: I see, and, and, what about sport?

Soc: Well, the results here are a bit surprising, er, as far as outdoor sports and games are concerned, 38% often take part, um, so *(3)* _____, outdoor sports are really still quite popular.

Int: Mm, mm, um, what other activities are there that teenagers do?

Soc: Predictably, I think, as far as, er, particularly the girls are concerned, 39% of them say that they, er, like to go dancing, to dancehalls or discotheques, places like that, you know. Um, another 19% mention going to parties as a, as a, one of their favourite activities and 28% say that they often, um, play indoor games and sports *(4)* _____ their leisure time.

Int: Ah, ha. Um, we seem to think nowadays that teenagers, er, have lots more money than they used to have, er, is that true?

Soc: Er, very much so, um, one of the reasons is that nowadays teenagers can earn quite a lot, er, taking part-time jobs, particularly at weekends and then again parents are much better off and, and so the children even when they do earn some spare pocket money (5) _____ _____ as in the past to contribute to *(yes)* the overall household expenses. *(mm, mm)*. Um, interesting this question money because, um, in the past, you know, it was very, it was quite easy really to differentiate between a middle-class and a working-class child, er, one could tell by the comparative poverty of, of the working-class child but often it's the other way round nowadays in that, er, the working-class child frequently goes out to work earlier and, and is earning, er, before the middle-class child has managed to, er, get out and put some money in his pocket because (6) _____ _____ and so the position is somewhat reversed.

Int: I see, and wh . . . , what do teenagers spend their money on?

Soc: Well, er, for sixteen-year-old working-class girls who are not in full-time education virtually 40% of their money goes on clothes and, and cosmetics, in fact that's the biggest single item.

Int: And, er, for boys?

Soc: Oh, no question here. The biggest outlay is, is on cigarettes and drink, um, about 25% of, of their income.

Int: Ah, ha, um, I suppose it's true to say that teenage years (7) _____, er, um, fraught with problems — the age of sixteen somehow seems to be a particularly difficult age. Um, does this survey throw any light on this?

Soc: Er, it certainly does. Um, in the survey the parents of sixteen-year-olds were given a list of characteristics thought to be typical of, of sixteen-year-olds, for example, 'restlessness', 'bullying', 'disobedience', things like that, er, (8) _____ _____ which of these were typical of their own children's behaviour as far as they were able to judge from their behaviour at home *(mm, mm)*. The most common characteristic which, er, was quoted was 'a tendency to be solitary', um, after that there was, er, 'irritable, being quick to fly off the handle' and the third was 'fussy and over-particular'.

Int: What about some of those, er, characteristics (9) _____ just now, um, 'bullying', er, 'disobedient' and the like?

Soc: Er, surprisingly, I think, few parents actually said that they found their children either 'bullying' or 'frequently disobedient'. I suppose, then, er, they wanted in some way to protect their children, you know, not give a bad impression of their behaviour.

Int: Ah, ha.

Unit 17　A Foreign Correspondent

Interviewer: I wonder if you could tell me, er, who you work for?

Foreign Correspondent: I work for Reuter's news agency, which is one of the four large world-wide news agencies, sending news to newspapers, television stations, radio stations, and to the business community, world-wide.

Int: Um, how long have you been working for, for Reuter's?

FC: I've been working for Reuter's 15 years.

Int: Is this, er, the first country (1) _____, em, for them, or not?

FC: No, I've worked off and on in about 40 countries for Reuter's (2) _____ _____ mainly. I started in West Africa in Ghana, I then went to Singapore in South East Asia and then the neighbouring country to the north, Malaysia, and after that I went back to West Africa, to Nigeria, and after a period in London, I have been in Portugal for the past two years, and I'm preparing to go — hopefully — to Korea, that's in Asia again, between Japan and China.

157

Int: Em, how does, how does one normally get into journalism in the first place? I mean, is there a single route into, into the profession, or, or, well . . . ?

FC: Well, the traditional method was that one joined one's little local weekly newspaper and then moved on to a regional, er, evening or daily paper, one of the newspapers in the provinces, *(3)* _____ _____ Fleet Street and working for a Fleet Street daily, one of the national newspapers of Britain. Of course, there are some people who went from, er, their local newspaper into radio or television, but that is the, the old-fashioned route and is still done today . . . but . . .

Int: Is that . . . that's *(4)* _____ as well?

FC: No, I didn't do it, I had a rather mixed career before then, em, but let me digress and say that most people now, recruiting for Reuter's and for a lot of the major newspapers in England, are graduates and they have a graduate trainee scheme, and they go straight for, from university to do a, an apprenticeship, if you like, *(mm, mm)* at the newspaper of, of their choice.

Int: Does this mean that there are undergraduate studies which, er, prepare people for journalism, or are there certain undergraduate degrees which, em, a newspaper *(5)* _____, as, as, necessary background, or desirable background?

FC: No, there aren't, er, er, there isn't a specific, er, B.A. Journalism, Bachelor of Arts degree in Journalism, *(6)* _____ _____ in the United States, for example, and in other countries. In England, erm, the tendency is to do a straight degree, obviously in Reuter's for foreign correspondents, we are particularly interested in languages, although many of our people have, em, science degrees, business degrees, any sort of degrees—mathematician, I am a zoologist by qualification, *(7)* _____ they take all sorts of people. *(mm, mm)* But what normally happens is, erm, that

one does an extra course, either through some of the big newspaper foundations, like the Thomson Foundation, they have courses in Cardiff — or through the National Union of Journalists who have courses at technical colleges on the particular disciplines required in journalism — law, for example.

Int: I imagine that, er, pressure for jobs is, is, quite high. I mean, is there a, is it a, erm, *(8)* _____ particularly lucky to, to get in, are you, is it like, you know, breaking through as a film-star or something?

FC: I think that's a slight exaggeration, we're not really film-stars. We're the faceless ones, representing the 'Fourth Estate', the ordinary man in the street, we hope. No, there is competition, but one must put it in perspective, because there's competition for all jobs in England at the moment, and in many other countries, because of unemployment. But we do take in Reuter's, for example, about 20 graduates each year, and we have applications from up to 400. *(mm, mm)* *(9)* _____.

Int: Thinking about your, your job here in Portugal, um, are you completely free to, to choose the stories that you write about, or are you given directives?

FC: Well, we have guidelines of course, I mean, we don't write stories *(10)* _____ _____, because we are serving, in a free enterprise situation, a market and we don't write things that no one is interested in and therefore, what are Reuter readers interested in? When you think that, em, 60% of Reuter's income comes from Europe, obviously, er, European considerations — what the European newspapers, radio stations and television stations are interested in — is of major importance.

Int: Ah, ha. Um, so you haven't got the British public in mind when you're writing? It's a much wider audience.

FC: No, we are a British-based news agency, but we *(11)* _____ just as British. We are a, em, a non-profit, er dispersing, *ie.* we don't give

158

money away to shareholders, but we are owned by the newspapers of Britain, Australia and New Zealand, so we look on ourselves as, *(12)* _____, a Commonwealth news agency, based in London.

Int: But your reporting is bought by, em, many countries outside.

FC: Oh, most certainly. We couldn't do without our markets throughout Africa and, em, Asia and South America. We have large services there, and, for example, in Europe we do provide a service in French, of French news for Frenchmen; and in Germany, a, a service in German of German news for Germans.

Int: Is there a conflict at any time between what you yourself would like to write and what you feel you have to write *(13)* _____, er, in the employment of Reuter's?

F.C.: There . . . We are guided by the strictest legal laws of libel and these are the British laws. For example, em, I cannot interview a, er, person who is in, in court, er, on a major charge, like they can in the United States, for example. No, I have to, er, *(14)* _____ the strict British legal system. Em, there are stories that come up which you have to say, here is a story . . . if I send this, the, my host country will probably want me to leave on the next plane, er, the ruling on this sort of story — and they come up fairly frequently — is, er, that one consults, and one's editors in London will decide, er, whether or not the story is sufficiently important to jeopardise the Reuter man in the, in the country concerned. Because our subscribers, the people who buy our service, *(15)* _____ _____ their own correspondent in to do an exposé, or some rather, er, strong story which will get them in bad odour with the government, but they want the agency man to be there through thick and thin, just in case the big story breaks.

Unit 19 Children and Television

Housewife: What do I think of television? Um, um, well, um, it keeps, keeps the family at home, the kids, the kids don't go out at night so much now, they come straight in from school most of them, they run in and straight, well the television's on when they come in, erm, *(1)* _____ _____ meself during the afternoon. Er, well it's company really and, er, well, then the kids come home, they eat their tea, they don't, I have no trouble with them eating their tea because they, em, they just . . . well, they don't even look *(2)* _____ _____, they just, they just sit down and, erm, they eat it and they like the programmes and, and it keeps them quiet while I'm cooking the tea for, for their dad when he comes home an hour later and *(3)* _____ _____ when the news is on when he comes in, and, er and the news is on or perhaps the football match or something, er, they have to be quiet then, they're not very interested in that themselves, they like the, the cartoons and things but, em, yeah, well, I think television's great, er, we get on much better in, in the house now, we, um, well, we've got, we've got things to talk about, erm, you know, if, if I miss a programme, er, if I'm cooking or something in the kitchen, I miss a bit of what's going on, I mean I have the door open so I can hear, but if I ha . . . , if I miss a bit then they, *(4)* _____, and then perhaps later or perhaps the next day we'll have a chat about it, you know. It gives us something to talk about really. Um, I don't think it hurts the kids, I don't think it's a problem, you know, like, er, it stops them, makes their eyes go funny or something, I don't think it's a problem like that. I think they, I think they er, no, no, I don't think it's a problem at all. They've . . . they've learned a lot from television, I think, um, yeah, my kids, they, they're always piping up with questions and *(5)* _____ from the television. Course the problem is later on at night when me and the old man want to watch ourselves on our own for a bit, but, you know, we have the kids hanging around outside the door and, you put them in bed but they're sneaking back down the stairs again to, you know, watch what we're watching and stuff, you know. Um, but, no, I don't really think that's a big problem 'cos *(6)* _____ a spanking and put them back in the bed. But, no, I think it's really good, I don't know what we'd do without a television really, em, provides background, you know.

Unit 22   A Change is as Good as a Rest

Interviewer: Um, the old saying has it that, er, a change is as good as a rest, er, for, er, people who are planning their holidays, do you think this is still true?

Travel Agent: Er, it depends on the individual, of course, but as a general rule, yes, I think that's so. *(mm, mm)* Um, for example, a man who has a very demanding job, who has to really over-exert himself, er, like a big store manager *(yeah)* well, he would most likely gain the most benefit from a good, quiet, relaxing holiday *(1)* _____, perhaps on a beach somewhere, er, remote from a city, while his wife, er, well, she would probably want a hotel holiday, wouldn't she, where there's no housework, where she could get away from cooking and be served and waited on *(yes)* for a change . . .

Int: Yes, that's, that's fairly, fairly predictable, isn't it?

TA: Yes, there is always a problem of course, you know, there are a lot of people who fall into a, the trap of going on a holiday which is just, er, basically a continuation or an extension of their normal daily life *(um, um)*. For example, you get a salesman who spends his week

driving from city to city all over Britain living in, virtually in his car and then chooses to take his car on a driving holiday through Europe, well, he has a company car *(yes, yes)* of course and doesn't cost him very much, er, but *(2)* _____ is that this is going to indul . . . involve him in all sorts of extra strains and problems, he's got to cope with different languages, he then has the problem of finding accommodation when he gets to the other end, he has to learn about the new rol . . . road rules and regulations so really *(3)* _____ that he suffers in normal, everyday life.

Int: And his wife?

TA: Well, same problem, isn't it? Um, she spends her week cooking and cleaning and looking after children and yet very frequently she's going to choose a self-catering holiday in a caravan or a cottage, er, *(4)* _____ exactly the same work that she does at home except that, erm, she's working in unusual surroundings and probably has to operate in more difficult *(more difficult, yes, yes)* circumstances.

Int: So in other words, I mean, neither of them would, would come back feeling rested or *(that's right)* the advantage of having a holiday.

TA: *(5)* _____ to get a rest.

Int: Yes, yes. Um, what general tips would you, would you be able to give about, er, planning holidays?

TA: Well, I think the, the first thing really is that *(6)* _____ a holiday of, that's worth anything, you've got to get completely away from your everyday environment. Erm, a businessman, for example, has got to cut himself off completely from his work *(yes)* and from his colleagues, he must be incommunicado, people shouldn't be able to be able to get in touch with him over business problems. Um, another thing is that, if your, if you have children and *(7)* _____ I think it's a good idea for them to have separate holidays, this gives the parents that bit of freedom er, be together for a change, er, which they can't do for most of the year . . .

Int: *(8)* _____ cater for the, the children.

TA: That's right. Absolutely. They can plan a holiday that suits them and at the same time it gives this, the children this feeling of independence which must be good for them in the long run *(um, um)*, erm . . .

Int: This would only be the case with older children though.

TA: Yes, I er, well, I don't know, it changes of course from child to child *(9)* _____ fourteen, fifteen probably might be old enough for some of them *(yeah, yeah)*. Er, a third thing, I think, worth thinking about is, is money, um, too many people, it seems to me, plan holidays without taking account of *(10)* _____ or what their resources are and of course they finish up running short and this ruins what otherwise would have been a good holiday and it's completely counter-productive. So plan a holiday in a place that you know you can afford and perhaps leave a bit le- over for those little extras *(11)* _____ into account *(ah, ha)*.

Unit 24 Living Collectively

Interviewer: What do you think? Do you think there are any viable alternatives to the traditional set-up?

Judy Sheppard: Yes, I do, um, living collectively, for example, not necessarily in the 'hippie self-sufficiency' model of the late sixties, um, but living, particularly in the case of single-parent families, erm, er, collectively so that one, one shares child-care *(1)* _____ with, with a career which one may have started and, and still be interested in *(yeah)* in keeping up.

Int: But I mean this, I would imagine, would throw up a whole range of addi-

tional problems or different problems from, er, the traditional nuclear family set-up. What would these be, do you think?

JS: Most certainly. Ob . . . the obvious problems of living in a group, I mean, people, some of you may have had the experience of coming from a large family and, er, the problem *(2)* _____ _____, so many people around all the time and then this kind of agreement to compromise. There are financial problems living with a variety of people who are earning a variety of salaries — people who may not be earning anything to people who are earning astronomical amounts of money and dividing expendit . . ., practical domestic expenditure . . .

Int: But do you think that these people would in fact come together in the first place — those extremes?

JS: Ah, well, I think there's obviously got to be an initial commitment to the idea and certain, I mean, I hate, I hate to say rules because that makes it sound like a kind of tremendously regimented establishment *(3)* _____ a definite kind of commitment in terms of collective responsibility *(yeah)*. Certainly, I mean, both, both financially and in terms of sharing *(mm, mm)*, er, domestic task-jobs around the house, the workload, the childcare, etc. etc. plus the ob . . . the obvious difficulties of different kind, different kinds of ideas about how one brings up one's, one's children, which *(4)* _____, I mean, obviously there's no hard and fast rule but certainly there's got to be some kind of channel of communication between this group *(yeah)* of people.

Int: But in a way many of those exist, perhaps in a different form, in a nuclear family . . . situation, as well.

JS: Yeah, um, but I think the nuclear family is, is, is, is probably far more structured in terms of, of mo . . . ., the hierarchy of father — breadwinner, mother — staying at home and, and children who are necessarily dependent both economically and emotionally on,

161

on, on the parents *(yeah)* and so I, I don't think *(5)* _____ *(yeah)* although there are similarities.

Int: Okay, well, there are some of, er, the problems that you've mentioned but wh . . . what do you, what would you list as some of the advantages . . . of, er, collective living?

JS: Um, well, the obvious sort of supportive structure of living with people going through the same kind of experience as oneself so *(6)* _____ bottled up one, one has the opportunity to actually work through various things, work through one's job, work through looking after kids with, with other people in su . . . which, which will obviously kind of facilitate, particularly in the case of women, being able to maintain some semblance of independence in terms of keeping one's job as well as fulfilment in terms of, of, of having children and providing a sort of safe, strong, secure base for these children to grow up *(mm, mm)* within. There's the obvious joy *(7)* _____ the menial household chores like sweeping the stairs, which are not just a burden for you but can again be, be pooled in terms *(yes)* . . . plus the whole idea of actually pooling resources both financially plus being able to provide, if you are living with a lot of different people, one, one has obviously got resources so that one has more space, one can provide kids with a garden, etc. etc. etc.

Int: I mean, on balance, um, which one would you come out in favour of, I mean, it seems as though *(8)* _____ as, er, a system which might come into operation if the nuclear family breaks down, but do you see this as an alternative way of, er, living, er, with married couples, or couples living together, or do you see it as a system which could come into operation for a single parent, um?

JS: Er, I see it actually as a combination of the two. Obviously there would be difficulties and possible sort of emotional friction if there were couples plus single

people but certainly I *(9)* _____ _____ could actually work, again if it was actually talked through, um, and, and people were actually aware of, of, of what they were doing and what their responsibility to the group as a whole was. Ob . . . obviously there's got to be room for individual relationships both with one's own children as well as other people's children plus the individual adults with . . . within the group.

Unit 25 Getting Away from It All

Interviewer: It's becoming increasingly common these days for people to . . . em . . . throw up their jobs and move away from big towns and I, I gather this is your, your position as well. What is it exactly you're, you're planning to do?

Mike: Well, we're living in a sort of suburb in South London at the moment, *(yes)* and er, you know, *(1)* _____, commuting into, into town *(yes)* em, on the bus.

Teresa: We both work in town *(ah, ha)*.

M: Spending a lot on the bus. I work in a sports shop em . . .

T: And, em, I'm a draughtswoman in a, a large engineering company right in the centre of town *(mm, mm)* and I find the travelling, well it's very, very wearing, I mean, we, we both get home late in the evening, we hardly see each other at all.

M: And *(2)* _____, you know, and exchanged bits of news about the day *(yes, yes)* the day's almost over really.

Int: How *(3)* _____ these jobs?

T: Well, I've been working now for eight years.

M: Yeah, I did one or two other things, I've been in the shop for about six now, we've been married for the last three.

T: And we've been saving for those last

three years really, *(4)* _____ towards this . . .

Int: So this is, this is not something that has suddenly cropped up, you've had this idea of moving away from the city, er, for some time.

M: Yeah, sure. I think, from my point of view anyway, *(yeah)* er, the, the real reason I wanted to get out was that I, *(5)* _____ this great interest in, in the outdoor life, you know, I do a lot of climbing and walking in my spare time and frankly from London you've got to drive so far to get anywhere . . . em . . . that it, it . . .

Int: And it's expensive I suppose.

M: Absolutely, yeah. And Teresa, well . . .

T: Well, I, I mean, I share Mike's enthusiasm for outdoors at least I'm, *(6)* _____ on the facilities that London has to offer, so there's really no point in my living near it . . . em . . . and besides that I really would like to have a chance to paint, I mean, being a draughtswoman is, is okay but there's absolutely no chance of using one's initiative at all and I'd like to have, have the time to, to do something a little bit more artistic.

Int: Yes, what exactly are you going to do? Where are you going?

M: Well, we, we bought this, this cottage actually, er, it, it's in a national park, in, in a village and it's a place where a lot of, er . . . a lot of tourists go, a lot of, er, er walkers, *(7)* _____ or spending their holidays there . . .er it's, it's, well, it's a shell, isn't it really? er . . .

T: It is ⎰ at the moment, yes ⎱
M: ⎱ at the moment, so ⎰

Int: So this is . . .

T: I mean, I'm hoping to be able to actually you know, design, er, an adaptation, part . . . , I mean, it's just about liveable in at the moment *(yes)* but we want to make that part better and then perhaps, well, we hope to build a sort of area where Mike *(8)* _____ .

Int: I see.

M: So I thought with my experience in the, you know, in, in the trade, *(9)* _____

_____ in the last few years.

Int: Yes, yes.

M: That we could, er, build a little, er, in, in, a little shop into the design and I could sell climbing equipment, camping stuff, er, and that kind of thing which would give us a fairly firm financial basis.

Int: Mm, mm. Sounds lovely. Um, what, what changes are you, sort of, most looking forward to, I mean, in contrast with the, with your life-styles over these last few years?

T: Well, mainly being together, really, because we hardly see each other at all living a suburban life, so *(10)* _____ _____, we don't know whether it will but that's, that's the first thing, I think, isn't it?

M: I think, yeah, I think it, it should, well, it, well, we're going to be doing different things basically. Teresa's going to be working on her art . . . stuff and I'm going to be man . . ., trying to manage this shop but we're both going to be around, em, so we've got different things that concern us and different things to talk about *(11)* _____ a lot more.

Int: A lot of people have these ideas, I imagine most people have them at one time or another in their lives but they never get to the point of being a reality. I mean, you're now going to do this. It's a, it's a big step, I mean you must have some fears, some worries.

T: Mm, yes, I mean, we do, we realise it's a, it's a risk, really, the main, the main fears are economic ones, aren't they?

M: Yeah.

T: To start with.

M: I think we're fairly, you know, *(12)* _____ fairly well on the ground, em, it's not going to be easy for me, em, I've got a lot of good friends in London and, unlike Teresa, I actually enjoy some of the facilities that the city offers as well *(yes)* I mean, *(13)* _____ _____ for example. Um, and I've got some good friends and, you know, we're going to go up there and really

163

have to make a whole new social circle and, er, the, the village is still basically rural *(yeah, yeah)* and, er, well, we've been used to the city and, er, you know, values are different and it's not going to be easy to, er, to find friends who have the same kind of interests and . . .

Int: What's, what have, what's been the reaction of your, your, your relatives and friends?

M: Well, I think *(14)* _____ with my parents because, em, I mean, we are, one of the things we, we plan to do when we've, when we've set up the, the house, the cottage and the business is, is to start a family and my parents are still in London *(yes)* and in fact they were just on the doorstep and I think *(15)* _____ when, you know, they could just pop . . .

Int: It would have been handy for you as well.

M: Pop round the corner, yeah, pop round the corner and, and see the children, well, erm . . .

T: I mean, we feel that it would be a good place to bring up children, basically much better than in the city, but on the other hand there are, there are lots of anxieties around there, we don't know what the school is, schooling is going to be like, I mean, at the moment *(16)* _____ all the time, so that, that is a worry, um, I don't have parents to worry about but, but, Mike does. Friends, we, we think, I mean, so many of our friends are, are fond of climbing anyway. . . .

Int: You'll be inundated with weekend visitors, yes.

T: We think they'll probably come. Yes, yes I think we might even see too much of them.

Int: Ha, ha, um, have you given any thought to er, the possibility *(17)* _____, I mean, what might you do if, if it doesn't come off?

T: Well, we've thought about it, haven't we?

M: Yeah.

T: I mean basically we can always go back, I suppose, em, but I think we would feel

that very much as a failure.

M: I think *(18)* _____ give, give it a fairly hard try.

Int: Well, the best of luck.

M: Thanks very much.

Unit 30 Who's Afraid of the Silicon Chip?

Interviewer: I suppose it's true to say that most people are still largely unaware of the effect that the silicon chip is going to have on their daily lives. Um, I wonder *(1)* _____ .

Technological Expert: Yes, er, well let's take the average, middle-income family as an example, um, and perhaps concentrate on one object say, the, the television set.

Int: And see what changes will, will, will happen to that.

TE: Yes, yes exactly. Um, some facilities we can take as, er, I suppose, standard at the moment, or *(2)* _____ standard, um, for example, using a video recorder, um, action replays, freezing, um, recording several programmes simultaneously and so on and of course, also, say, using, um, the television set for playing television games *(yes)* I mean, all this is either standard or soon will be in, in a number of countries.

Int: Ah, ha, okay, I mean, as you say, this is something we're, we're becoming more and more familiar with at the moment. Er, what other developments *(3)* _____, to take place?

TE: Ah, yes, well, um, television sets will have a keyboard rather like a typewriter and of course this does open up quite a number of rather exciting, er, possibilities.

Int: Ah, ha, for example?

TE: Well, shopping is a very good example. Um, soon I think the electronic mail order system will come into being. Um, here *(4)* _____ on a screen, you know, by pushing keys, a, a list of items that you want to buy. You'll be able to compare prices in different shops, um, you know, choose the items you want and then press certain keys and place your order. Then by giving a credit card number you can pay automatically as well.

Int: So the shopping can be done, er, from home.

TE: That's exactly it, yes. And, um, all sorts of information, um, you know, stored, can be summoned up on a screen by pushing keys. *(5)* _____ for each item. Um, let's take an example; um, we have a certain code for what's on in London, and another one, say, for booking tickets for a theatre or cinema and yet another one for, um, lists of second-hand cars for sale and so on, and of course houses on the market. In fact, um, the present GPO's Prestel System is just like this.

Int: So you can, erm, find out by pressing these keys a whole lot *(yes)* of information which is stored in some sort of bank, I suppose.

TE: That's, that's it, right.

Int: Well, so far *(6)* _____ is for, if you like, convenience or entertainment purposes. Um, are there any more, let's say, serious applications that the silicon chip is going to have?

TE: Yes, certainly. Let's take work possibilities, um, for example, a salesman gets home after a hard day's work, feeds in information on his day's work through the keyboard to the firm's computer and almost instantly receives instructions on screen for the following day. *(mm, mm)* Um, of course also, um, *(7)* _____ _____ as a work-base and it makes it much easier, um, I think this is particularly important, um, for those who are, say, housebound anyway. I think a good example: parents with young children or disabled people.

Int: Yes, yes, and, er, presumably some in, in the field of education this is, *(8)* _____ a lot of developments there.

TE: Oh, vast number. Um, it'll be possible to follow courses on videocassette, um, these can be played when and as often as you like and, of course, most important, you can tap sources of immediate information through the keyboard. It would be quite possible, er, to have a computerised encyclopaedia available *(ah, ha)*, er, so if you want to know facts and figures about, say, Chad — good example — *(9)* _____ ____ the appropriate, er. . . .

Int: Code . . .

TE: Code, that's right, and then instantly you'll get the information you want.

Int: I see.

TE: And so it goes on. Um, just one more example. Um, a TV set will have a printer attached so a friend, say, could tap out a letter on his keyboard *(10)* _____ on your screen. And if you want what's called 'a hard copy', er, the printer could produce one.

Int: Er, printed out?

TE: That's it, yes, so in other words you'll be, if you like, the GPO of the future.

165

Answer Key

Because many questions in the Units invite a range of different opinions it is impossible to give definitive answers here. The Answer Key limits itself to providing answers to those questions which are based on fact rather than opinion (denoted by the symbol Ⓚ). Often the answers may be expressed in many alternative and equally acceptable ways.

1 First Impressions

B1

2 (i) *a* auburn: reddish-brown
       b sandy: yellowish-red
       c mousey: dull brown
       d chestnut-coloured: deep reddish-brown
       e greying: turning grey (with age)
       f fair: light in colour (less so than 'blonde')

   (ii) | d | b | a | c |
         |---|---|---|---|
         | 1 | 2 | 3 | 4 |

3 (i) (i) skinny   (iii) slender
        (ii) slight   (iv) slim
   (ii) (i) stout   (iii) thick-set
        (ii) plump   (iv) podgy

2 Body Shapes and Behaviour

A2 1 ectomorph   4 mesomorph
       2 endomorph   5 endomorph
       3 mesomorph   6 ectomorph

B1

Endomorphs	Mesomorphs	Ectomorphs
complacent	*dominant*	*responsive*
tolerant	*aggressive*	*controlled*

C *(i)* the opposite point of view
(ii) an impressive physical appearance
(iii) enjoying a series of successes
(iv) has an enormous amount of energy and initiative

3 Friend of a Friend

C1

Speaker	Connection with Bill Evans	Problems of staying (if any)	Outcome of phone call
Cathy O'Brien	*Bill and Cathy were at university together.*	*Cathy wants no contact with any friend of Bill Evans who caused a lot of trouble in the past. No room. Husband would be very upset.*	*Terry's request is refused.*
Norman Bowes	*Bill used to share a flat with Norman's brother.*	*Norman's wife is ill in bed. They have two children.*	*Norman and his wife will talk it over and Terry will phone again later.*
Jan Simpson	*Bill used to work at the Star and Garter (a local pub).*	*No serious problem, but apologetic about the state of the spare room.*	*Terry is to go to Jan's straight away.*

Gapped Tapescript

(1) been at university with you
(2) seems to have settled down
(3) when he wasn't wanted
(4) would be nice to meet
(5) don't feel that I'd
(6) he should have given you
(7) to have bothered you
(8) I knew him all that well
(9) it would be nice for me

(10) it might be possible
(11) might be able to give me
(12) have you got any other
(13) I'll tell you what I'll do
(14) I've been . . . for a couple of years
(15) I think he'll probably stay
(16) you might be able to
(17) I'm quite used to sleeping
(18) actually it's not at all difficult

4 Posture

None

5 Faces

Ⓣ A1

	Pictures
First description	(b)
Second Description	(e)
Third Description	(f)
Fourth Description	(a)

Ⓣ B1

	First Description (Picture *b*)	Second Description (Picture *e*)	Third Description (Picture *f*)	Fourth Description (Picture *a*)
Eyes	×	dark and lively	*dark; attractive sparkle*	*warm; honest-looking*
Nose	*fairly small; rounded*	*on the small side; somewhat pointed*	not very large; rather broad	×
Mouth/Lips	small thin lips	×	×	rather thin lips
Hair	*dark; pushed to one side*	fairly dark	*dark; pushed to one side*	*long; dark; shiny*
Overall Appearance	not very striking; fresh-faced	*alert; intelligent; good-looking*	friendly and confident; over-confident?	attractive; rather angular
Build	*on the tall side; quite strong*	*rather short; neat; compact*	stocky; rather overweight	*quite tall and slim; probably skinny*
Personality	self-effacing; serious and reliable; fairly naive	*a lot of fun; ups and downs; a sharp temper*	*strong; jovial and good company; gets on well with opposite sex*	kind and reserved; not easy to know; good, reliable friend
Hobbies/ Interests	*reading; going for walks*	parties; fast cars	*eating out; watching sport*	*opera; gardening; home-loving*

Ⓣ Gapped Tapescript
(1) pushed to one side
(2) I would imagine that
(3) and could well have
(4) but one who doesn't easily tolerate
(5) I can imagine this person being
(6) As far as interests go
(7) all in all
(8) a home-loving sort

6 Elemental Truths

A2
(i) scatty
(ii) congenial
(iii) opinionated
(iv) impetuous
(v) long-suffering
(vi) moody
(vii) dreamy and dopey
(viii) spineless
(ix) supportive
(x) penny-pinching
(xi) smug
(xii) two-faced

B1   Fire [I]   Earth [III]   Air [IV]   Water [II]

7 Doodling

A2 Analysis of I

Self Image

If your partner has drawn a charming or comic figure or face it shows good nature, a sense of humour, diplomacy.
An ugly figure shows he/she has difficulty getting close to other people.
A sun indicates a strong, dominant, self-confident personality.
A flower is feminine. It shows care about surroundings and appearance.
A regular and balanced design means the person is always wondering if he/she left the gas on or forgot to lock the front door.
An eye denotes pride, a suspicious nature.
Anything else — you'll have to work it out for yourself.

Home

If something is drawn within the box then interests lie in the home.
If something is drawn outside it, then interests lie outside the home.
The unattached may make nest-like symbols (fire-place, house, window) and put something in the box to indicate their idea of home (champagne glass, bed).
Drawings both inside and outside the box show ambivalence (which is normal).
If the box has been made into a grotesque face, it shows fear of home and/or marriage.

Friendship

Most people make several separate and distinct shapes in this square. Drawing many shapes indicates many friends.

Shapes within the two lines indicate friends restricted to an in-group.
Shapes outside the two lines indicate acquaintances, casual friends.
A single line suggests the person is reserved, self-centred.
A coffin or box means the person is lonely and moody.
Girls who make parallel lines are romantic, have mostly male friends.
Men who make circular shapes have mostly girl friends.
Criss-crossing or X's inside the lines indicate a person who is only interested in close, lasting friendships.

 Sex

If this symbol has been used as a solid shape (building, animal's neck, etc), it shows a healthy, uninhibited attitude towards sex.
If the space between the lines is blank and obscures the symbol, it shows modesty and shyness about sex.
A tree indicates an identification of sex with marriage, home and children.
If there is fruit on the tree then the person is extremely keen on children.
If it's a rocket — well!

 Confidence

If the person draws above the line it shows he/she is well-adjusted. A ship is common.
If the ship is moving it shows great security.
If there are drawings below the line it means the opposite.
If there are drawings above and below the line — which part of the drawing is more important?
If your partner has drawn someone drowning he/she is worried about the future.
If he/she has made a chain or a pattern out of the centre line then he/she is hard-working and hardly ever makes a mistake.

 Main Interest

You can work this out for yourself.
If your partner has drawn a person of the same sex it shows that he/she is mainly interested in himself/herself.
Landscapes or still lifes indicate artistic ability.
If this square has been left blank the person should take up a hobby.

Analysis of II

Maturity

If these circles are closed, it shows the need for approval and protection.

How tightly are they closed? This indicates the degree to which the person is still influenced by what he learnt as a child.

If the circles aren't closed, it shows independence, ambitions and hopes projected into the future.

If the person has drawn an ear, he/she has a secret.

If she/he has made a cup it shows a loving maternal (or paternal) disposition.

Competition

Noughts and crosses in this square show a competitive nature.

If a winning game is drawn it shows your partner is a winner, or at least aggressive. If he/she has made a winning game by cheating, he/she is tricky and probably rich.

Men usually win with X's, women with circles.

If the symbol is obscured it shows your partner is passive and uncompetitive.

Girls often make a box or a home symbol showing 'wifely' qualities.

Some people will play the game with their own symbols (not X's or circles). These people are aggressive individualists who secretly wish to conform.

Aspiration

An arrow headed for the target shows an ability to work for a specific goal.

If there are other lines or arrows pointing to the target, it shows the person is ambitious but faced with a choice of goals.

If the symbol is obscured by turning it into something else (bird, wagon, lollipop) it shows a scatty, rebellious and imaginative character.

Discipline

If your partner accepts the symbol and has made a geometric design duplicating the square, he/she is able to accept discipline and work with other people in an organisation.

If your partner fights the black square and has made a curved irregular design, he/she tends to be stubborn. Either a trouble-maker or a potential genius or both.

If there are some square and some round shapes, your partner is confused and should start a new romance, change flats, get a new car. Or something.

Social Adaptability

If the shape of the symbol is echoed in the drawing (moon, round face, sunrise) it shows ability to get on with various types of people socially.

If the person has fought the symbol and made ugly or squarish shapes, it shows difficulty in mixing easily at parties and a tendency to smoke, drink or bite finger nails as a nervous habit. Also this person may be possessive in relationships.

Imagination

The dots in this square are a challenge to many people. If the dots have been used as part of a specific picture (bird, seed, rabbit tail, ants) it shows imagination.

If the dots have been obscured by drawing a solid circle around or through them, it shows a practical and logical nature.

If there is nothing in this square it shows lack of imagination and a willingness to lend people money.

8 Making New Friends

None

9 Give Us our Daily Drugs

A1

Drug Takers	1	2	3	4	5
Futures	E	D	A	C	B

B1
- *(i)* make ends meet
- *(ii)* bedridden
- *(iii)* brought down
- *(iv)* a cure
- *(v)* stick to
- *(vi)* cut himself off from

2
- *(i)* left university before completing his course
- *(ii)* a (simple) place to live in
- *(iii)* performances or shows on one evening only — and then continuing to another place and another show
- *(iv)* for excitement

10 Sharing a Home

None

11 Housing

A1   *(i)*   b   *(iii)*   d   *(v)*   a

         (ii)   f   *(iv)*   e   *(vi)*   c

B1

	Present Type of Housing	Main Problems of Present Housing	Ideal Type of Housing	Main Features of Ideal Housing
Speaker I	*a small flat in a modern apartment block*	*short of space*	*a big older-style semi*	*space; bedroom for each child; 2 bathrooms; a playroom; a study or work-room; cellars; a garden*
Speaker II	*an attic in a large old Victorian house*	*very cramped*	*a small terrace-house*	*3 bedrooms; a study; a little bit of space to sit out in; a large kitchen; an extra room (a bedroom, a study, for renting)*
Speaker III	*a bedsitter in the middle of town*	*small; dingy, shabby furniture*	*a large open-plan studio flat on 3rd or 4th floor*	*light; french windows on to a verandah; painted white; big pictures on wall; lots of plants; kitchen with machines; fairly large bed-room*

Gapped Tapescript

(1) we're a bit short of space

(2) that we've always wanted

(3) having to join a queue

(4) so it would be useful

(5) that we would be looking for

(6) are combined

(7) tend to get in the way

(8) what I'd like to do

(9) that would release

(10) I'd like it to be

(11) I'd still like to be living

(12) I'd like it all to be

12 Your Neighbourhood

None

13 Travel to Work

A1   *1 a* increased   *b* decreased
    2 decreased
    3 increased
    4 over $\frac{4}{5}$

    5 (i)

1965	1972/73	1975/76
35%	*54%*	*59%*

    (ii)

1965	1972/73	1975/76
1.32	*1.27*	*1.27*

    6 1% rise in bicycling and walking to work

    7

Means of Travel	Main Users: Male/Female	Age Range	% of Users in Age Range
1 Public Transport (especially bus)	*Female*	*16–20*	*51%*
2a Car/Van/Lorry	*Male*	*30–59*	*64%*
2b Car/Van/Lorry	*Male*	*21–29*	*61%*
3 Bicycles	*Male*	*60–64*	*10%*
4 On Foot	*Female*	*60–64*	*37%*

14 Teenagers' Leisure and Pleasure

                                       Tape

A1   *(i)* Playing outdoor games and sports   2

               Reading books (not school books)   3

               Watching TV   1

    (ii)

Tape
b

    (iii)

Tape
c

	Tape
(iv) Fussy	3
Bullying	
Lazy	
Solitary	1

	Tape
Restless	
Disobedient	
Irritable	2
Bored	

B2   *(i)* 14,000   *(ii)* 1976

(iii)

	%
Playing Outdoor Games and Sports	38
Reading Books (not school books)	27
Watching TV	65
Going to Parties	19
Dancing at Discos	39
Playing Indoor Games and Sports	28

(iv) The working-class teenager was often visibly poorer.

(v) Nowadays often the opposite is true because working-class teenagers tend to go out to work earlier and earn some money.

(vi) The parents did not want to give a bad impression of their children's behaviour.

Gapped Tapescript

(1) this is backed up

(2) has been exaggerated

(3) surprisingly as I say

(4) as a way of spending

(5) are not expected

(6) he has to stay on at school

(7) have traditionally been considered

(8) they were asked to say

(9) that you mentioned

15   How Much Do You Know about Whales?

A1   *(i)* mammals

(ii) seas and certain tropical rivers and lakes

(iii) the creatures mentioned are: dolphins and porpoises

(iv) about 30 metres (just under 100 feet)

(v) 136,000 kilograms (150 tons)

(vi) planktonic organisms; fish and squid

(vii) 56 k.p.h. (36 m.p.h.)

(viii) smell?   No, little or none

sight?   Yes, at least excellent in porpoises

hearing?   Yes, excellent

taste?   Yes, probably well developed

(ix) the products mentioned are: oil, soaps, cosmetics and detergents

(x) a serious danger

B3

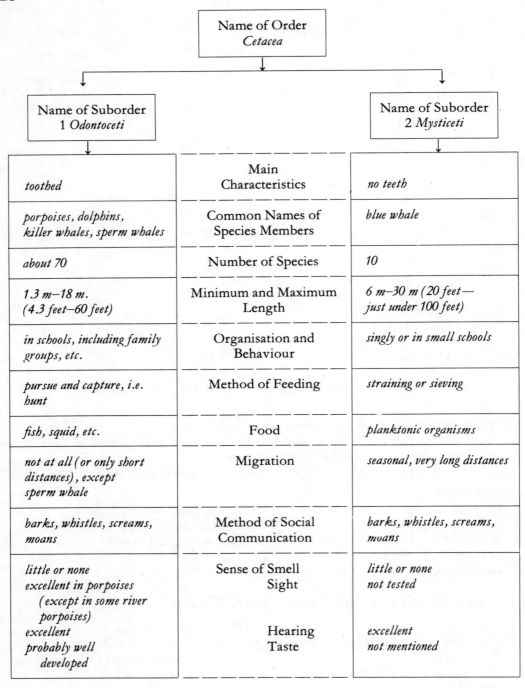

Odontoceti	Main Characteristics	Mysticeti
toothed	Main Characteristics	*no teeth*
porpoises, dolphins, killer whales, sperm whales	Common Names of Species Members	*blue whale*
about 70	Number of Species	*10*
1.3 m–18 m. (4.3 feet–60 feet)	Minimum and Maximum Length	*6 m–30 m (20 feet—just under 100 feet)*
in schools, including family groups, etc.	Organisation and Behaviour	*singly or in small schools*
pursue and capture, i.e. hunt	Method of Feeding	*straining or sieving*
fish, squid, etc.	Food	*planktonic organisms*
not at all (or only short distances), except sperm whale	Migration	*seasonal, very long distances*
barks, whistles, screams, moans	Method of Social Communication	*barks, whistles, screams, moans*
little or none *excellent in porpoises (except in some river porpoises)* *excellent* *probably well developed*	Sense of Smell Sight Hearing Taste	*little or none* *not tested* *excellent* *not mentioned*

16   What the Papers Said

A1

	Name	Job	Employer	Age	Main Part in the Story
1	Janet Parker	*photographer*	*Birmingham University*	*40*	*caught smallpox at Birmingham University and died*
2	Patrick Jenkin	*Secretary of State for Social Services*	*The Government*	*×*	*amended the foreword of the Government report*
3	Henry Bedson	*virologist*	*Birmingham University*	*48*	*killed himself as a result of Mrs Parker catching smallpox*
4	Clive Jenkins	*General Secretary of a Union*	*The Union*	*×*	*told the press about the Government report before its official publication*
5	Reginald Shooter	*Dean of a Medical College*	*St Bartholomew's Hospital, London*	*×*	*in charge of the committee which prepared the Government report*

3   *(i)* to allow the Secretary of State for Social Services to amend the foreword of the report

(ii) the court case was dismissed, i.e. it was unsuccessful

(iii) because of the recommendations it contained about the inspection of laboratories where work with dangerous pathogens is carried out

(iv) the University thought the report contained many errors

(v) it was claimed that there existed poor laboratory procedures and therefore virus particles were able to escape

(vi) through a duct (used for ventilation?) into the telephone room which she used several times a day.

B1

The Sun	*Daily Mail*
a grim report	a 215 page report
drawn up by an inquiry team led by top professor	strong objections by the university for its suppression
kept secret by the government for 18 months	'a blemished report'
was leaked by union boss	'retrial by innuendo through a discredited document'

C1

	The Times	The Sun	Daily Mail
	poor laboratory procedures	blundering incompetence	poor safety standards
		warnings were ignored	*inadequate staff training*
	a major breach in containment policy	*misleading reports about safety standards*	*inadequate sealing of ducts and inlets*
		not training staff properly	*insufficient sterilisation and disinfection*
		safety standards were so bad . . . instead of inside a safety cabinet	*use of dangerous viruses outside safety cabinets*
			poor laboratory standards
			the failure to use the safety cabinet
			the failure to use sealed containers . . .
			the practice of passing in and out of the smallpox room . . .

D

(i)	(ii)	(iii)
T	*S*	*M*

F The original *Times* article:

Woman wins appeal over struggle with police officer

Janet Lindley, aged 29, a student who was involved in a struggle with a policewoman who tried to remove her brassiere, won her appeal in the High Court yesterday against a conviction for assault.

The Court upheld her plea that magistrates at Exeter were wrong in finding her guilty of assaulting woman Policeconstable Fry in the execution of her duty.

Her appeal to the Queen's Bench Divisional Court was regarded by the police as an important test case on their right to search prisoners.

Lord Justice Donaldson and Mr Justice Mustill said they would quash Miss Lindley's conviction and give a full judgment at a later date, setting out guidelines on the scope of police rights.

Miss Lindley, of Clifton Hill, Exeter, was arrested accused of being drunk and disorderly. She was alleged to have scratched and kicked WP-c Fry during a struggle after the officer tried to remove her brassiere for her own protection, in case she tried to hang herself with it.

17 A Foreign Correspondent

B1 *1* Reuters   *2* four   *3* 15 years

4 40 countries but has been based in *(i)* Ghana *(ii)* Singapore *(iii)* Malaysia *(iv)* Nigeria and is leaving Portugal for Korea.

5

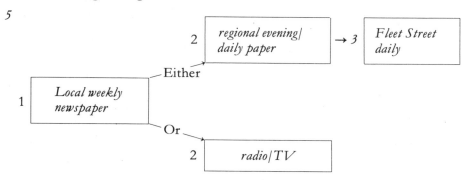

6 No

7 Graduates of Universities → Graduate Trainee Scheme — an apprenticeship

8 The United States
9 Languages
10 Zoology
11 *(i)* Through the big newspaper Foundations, e.g. The Thomson Foundation
   (ii) Through the National Union of Journalists
12 The ordinary man in the street
13 Up to 400; 20
14 Stories of interest to Reuters' readers and which have a good chance of being printed
15 Europe. Because 60% of Reuters' income comes from Europe
16 The newspapers of Britain, Australia and New Zealand
17 Britain
18 Reuters could not do without them
19 News in French for Frenchmen and news in German for Germans
20 British libel laws
21 When someone is in court on a major charge
22 He would consult his editors in London
23 The people who buy Reuters' news
24 Just in case there is a big story to write about

C *(i)* from time to time; not continuously
(ii) I did a variety of different jobs
(iii) the specific subjects which are most useful for a journalist
(iv) representing the common people, the average citizens (NB. an 'estate' in this sense means 'a political or social group'. The 'Three Estates of the Realm' refer to the Lords Spiritual, i.e. the Bishops in the House of Lords; the Lords Temporal, i.e. all the other Lords; and the Commons, i.e. the common

people. The journalist in the interview intended to refer to this latter group but instead mistakenly used the phrase 'the Fourth Estate' which is employed to refer jokingly to the press.

(v) we are given general advice

(vi) the laws protecting people from the publication of false statements which would damage someone's reputation

(vii) the necessary action to take (as laid down by the management of Reuters)

(viii) to put the Reuter correspondent in a dangerous or difficult position

(ix) make them unpopular in the eyes of the government

(x) to be there in all kinds of conditions, whether good or bad

Gapped Tapescript

(1) you've worked in
(2) but been based in about four
(3) before going to
(4) the way you did it
(5) will be looking for
(6) as you would get
(7) so you can see
(8) do you have to be
(9) Gives you an idea
(10) that don't get printed
(11) don't like to be described
(12) for want of a better word
(13) as a result of being
(14) be guided by
(15) they can always send

18 The Soap Opera

D1 The soap-opera serial called 'The Family' as described on page 69 has *not* been invented. It was shown on BBC TV between March–June 1974 and caused a considerable outcry. Viewers were told that 'for the next three months the Wilkins family will have a four-man TV crew to stay with them. All their actions will be filmed for a series of documentary programmes . . .'

The producer, Paul Watson, had great ambitions for the series and hoped that the events of the time, for example, a recent miners' strike and a closely-fought general election could be examined in the context of one family living its daily life. The Wilkins only earned a small fee from the programmes; their main reason for participating was that they believed that people like them rarely had a chance to be on TV. They thought that working-class life was misrepresented by TV and film companies.

When the first programme was shown, there was an audience of 7 to 10 million viewers. People reacted very critically to the whole venture —

'I cannot see the necessity of prying into the private lives of any family . . .'

'I can hardly believe it is an average family . . .'

'I am surprised the BBC showed such rubbish . . .'

were among some of the comments made.

19 Children and Television

A1 *(i)* 90%

(ii) 9 p.m.

(iii)

5–8 years	*24%*
9–11 years	*50%*

(iv) 62 mothers (out of 524)

(v) 74%

(vi) 8%

3 *(i)* parents exercise little or no control over their children's viewing

(ii) an indication should be given to parents in programme journals, etc. as to the suitability of programmes for children, e.g. 'R' = Restriction Recommended

(iii) whoever decides whether an 'R' is advisable might easily be influenced by what they personally like and dislike

B *(i)* negligence *(ii)* notional *(iii)* taste
(iv) onus *(v)* tricky *(vi)* trailer
(vii) smutty

Ⓣ **D1** The advantages of having a TV mentioned in the passage:
- it keeps the family at home
- it's company
- the family gets on much better at home
- they've got things to talk about
- the children learn a lot
- it provides background

Ⓣ **Gapped Tapescript**
(1) I have it on
(2) what they're eating sometimes
(3) they have to be quiet
(4) they'll tell me what's going on
(5) things that they've picked up
(6) you just give them

20 The Language of Advertising

A1 *(a)* 'Before and after' *(b)* Association of ideas
(c) Expertise *(d)* 'The camera never lies'
(e) Repetition *(f)* 'Science'
(g) 'Keeping up with the Joneses' *(h)* Brand names
(i) Key words *(j)* Guilt

21 Consumer Discrimination

A *(i)* because first-hand knowledge about the type and quality of materials, construction, performance, appearance and price is *not* often available to the consumer

(ii) reasoned argument and emotional responses

B1 *1* offensive to the standards of decency
2 abuse the trust of the consumer; exploit his lack of experience or knowledge
3 play on fear
4 lend support to acts of violence
5 capable of substantiation
6 mislead the consumer
7 misuse research results . . .
8 overestimate the value of goods
9 respect the principles of fair competition
10 unfairly attack or discredit other products
11 clearly distinguishable
12 refer to dangerous practices or manifest a disregard for safety
13 contain anything . . . which might result in harming them

C1 *1* anything which goes against what society considers respectable
2 exploit people by deliberately making them feel afraid
3 able to be supported or proven by providing facts
4 deliberately to misrepresent (by exaggeration, etc.) data obtained from university studies or from books, articles, etc.

22 A Change Is as Good as a Rest

Ⓣ **B1** *(i)* yes, as a general rule
(ii) *(a)* a quiet, relaxing holiday
(b) a hotel holiday with no housework
(iii) going on a holiday which is a continuation or extension of one's normal, daily life.

(iv)

Person	Holiday Chosen
salesman	*driving holiday*
his wife	*self-catering holiday*

(v) because they would be doing the things they do every day but in more difficult circumstances

(vi)

Environment	*get completely away from one's everyday environment*
Children	*older children should have separate holidays*
Money	*make sure you can afford the place you have chosen*

D1 *(i)* *soft, golden* sand; *warm, crystal-clear* sea
(ii) the weather is never bad (and it is therefore possible to perform the attractive outdoor activities all the year round)
'the constant companionship of a sun . . .'; 'joy in living . . . every day of the year'; 'it is always holiday time . . .'
(iii) the contrast between the attractions of the unspoilt countryside, the historical past etc., and those of the modern, sophisticated, cosmopolitan tourist world
(iv) it is possible to have the best of both worlds — to enjoy traditional things as well as all modern amenities

Ⓣ **Gapped Tapescript**
(1) far away from it all
(2) what he fails to realise
(3) he's just adding to the tensions
(4) she finds herself having to do
(5) they'd come back to work
(6) if it's going to be
(7) if they're just that bit older
(8) Instead of having to
(9) but I would have thought
(10) how much it's really going to cost them
(11) that you haven't taken

23 Is Being Single Still out of Line?

B1 (i) because she's 35 years old — halfway to 70 years old (the 'threescore years and ten' of the Bible)
(ii) because she has never married
(iii) they both got married in their twenties
(iv) her husband has another girl
(v) returning home alone after a supper party

3 (i)

people in the village (*para 2*)	pity
her mother (*para 5*)	*worry*
her sister (*para 6 and 7*)	*puzzlement and sometimes envy*
friends and acquaintances (*para 10*)	*embarrassment*

(ii)

her job (*para 3*)	Unexciting and undemanding but earns her money. At best, pleasant. At worst, petty and monotonous.
people's speculation about her (*para 9*)	*Sheila wishes people would stop speculating about her; she's tired of being regarded with patronising pity*
talking about being single (*para 10*)	*Sheila is happy to talk about it*
people's behaviour towards single women (*para 11*)	*Sheila is surprised that people still feel embarrassed about single women of her age*
loneliness (*para 13*)	*Sheila feels she is no lonelier than anyone else*

D1 (i) an oddity
(ii) taxing
(iii) petty
(iv) pitfalls
(v) pea-green
(vi) broods about
(vii) arch

2   *(i)* that she views marriage as a possible source of harm to herself
    (ii) for Sheila 'settled' means having a flat and paying into a pension and private health insurance scheme; for her mother, it means getting married and having a family
    (iii) they keep up the appearance of getting on with each other
    (iv) If Sheila tells people that she enjoys her lifestyle, they don't believe her; they think she's only saying it to try and compensate for the fact that she is not married.

24   Living Collectively

Ⓣ **B1**   *(i)* single-parent families
    (ii) *(a)* childcare is shared
         (b) possible to continue with a career
    (iii) *(a)* a lot of noise
         (b) financial problems
    (iv) the nuclear family is much more structured, *eg.* father earns money, mother stays at home and the children are economically and emotionally dependent on both
    (v) *(a)* living with people of similar beliefs
         (b) being able to share out the menial household chores
         (c) pooling resources
    (vi) for both couples and single-parent families

Ⓣ **C**   *(i)* agreement to adapt your lifestyle and behaviour to the other people you are living with
    (ii) responsibility is shared equally among every member of the collective
    (iii) the members of the collective have got to be able to talk to each other
    (iv) having people who understand you because they are going through the same kind of experience
    (v) an appearance of being independent
    (vi) each member of the collective does an equal share of the daily, routine work, *eg.* cleaning, shopping, etc.
    (vii) sharing the things that one has *eg.* finances, possessions, skills, etc.
    (viii) tension and difficulties between people

Ⓣ **Gapped Tapescript**
(1) as well as being able to continue
(2) of there being such a lot of noise
(3) but that there's got to be
(4) have all got to be worked out
(5) the problems are necessarily the same
(6) rather than having kind of a whole lot of problems
(7) of being able to share out
(8) we're looking at this
(9) think that kind of combination

25   Getting Away from It All

Ⓣ **A2**   *1* a suburb in South London
    2 Mike: works in a sports shop
       Teresa: a draughtswoman
    3 commuting/travelling is tiring
    4 Mike: 6 years
       Teresa: 8 years

5 Mike: interest in outdoor life
Teresa: also likes outdoor life; wants to paint
6 a cottage — in a village in a National Park
7 a shell — in very poor condition
8 design an adaptation of the cottage, to include a sports shop
9 spending more time together
10 Mike: manage the shop
Teresa: work in art
11 economic
12 theatre; has good friends
13 people have different values and interests
14 disappointed — they were hoping to be close to (future) grandchildren
15 they are no longer alive
16 schooling — closing village schools
17 enthusiastic
18 they would possibly go back to London

Ⓣ **B** *(i)* give up; resign from
(ii) travelling to and from work
(iii) tiring
(iv) happened unexpectedly
(v) with only the outer walls in good condition
(vi) fit to live in, but only just
(vii) with those people also working in the same job/profession
(viii) practical and realistic; know what to expect
(ix) living nearby
(x) make a quick, easy visit
(xi) see their friends too often
(xii) succeed

Ⓣ **Gapped Tapescript**
(1) the usual thing that involves
(2) by the time we've eaten
(3) long have you been doing
(4) we've been sort of working
(5) I've always had
(6) I'm not at all keen
(7) going up for the week-end
(8) can set up his own sports business
(9) I've built up a few contacts
(10) we hope it's going to work
(11) but we're going to be together
(12) we've got our feet
(13) I'm very fond of the theatre
(14) that was one of the problems
(15) they were looking forward to the time
(16) they're closing down village schools
(17) of it not working out
(18) we're prepared to

26 The Pneu Wave

A1 *(i)*

1	avoids cost and inconvenience of public transport
2	*keeps you in good shape*
3	*quicker over relatively short distances*
4	*contributes nothing unpleasant to the atmosphere*

(ii)

1	*proper parking facilities*
2	*cycle ways*
3	*space on trains for bikes (in and out of London during rush hour)*

(iii)

Type of bike	Cost	Suitable for
roadster (3 or 5 gears)	*minimum £75*	*short journeys, less than 5 miles — mainly flat*
derailleur (5 or 10 gears)	*£85*	*over 5 miles, hilly or gradual incline, cycling holiday*
folding bikes	*£90*	flat dwellers or families

B *(i)* compelling *(ii)* lobby *(iii)* saga
(iv) soar *(v)* manoeuvre

D1

Highway Code	(re)familiarise yourself
Routes	*plan to avoid congested areas or fast main roads*
Position on road	*about an arm's length from the kerb*
Clothing	*wear bright clothing*
Way to ride	*in a straight line*
Manoeuvres	*plan them with care*
Rain	*be extra careful*

E1 *(i)* kerb
(ii) drain cover
(iii) pot holes
(iv) bollard

2 *(i)* protected in a car
(ii) being inattentive; not paying attention
(iii) hesitate
(iv) suddenly and unexpectedly appear
(v) hindered; impeded; caused problems.

27 Vegetarianism

B1

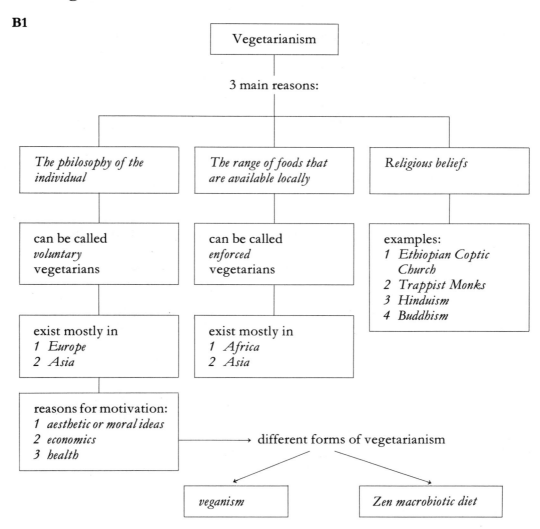

3

Nutrients	Intake in Relation to a Mixed Diet	Source
Calcium Vitamins B and C	higher	vegetables, fruit and nuts
Proteins	*similar*	*mixed cereals, vegetables*
Water	*higher*	*vegetables*
Fat	*lower*	*nuts, oils, vegetable fats*

C *(i)* gorge   *(iv)* affluence
    (ii) nutriment   *(v)* deplore
   (iii) eccentricity   *(vi)* nutrient

28   Schools with a Difference

A1

	Ordinary Boarding School	Summerhill School
Sleeping quarters	Dormitories	*Rooms*
Clothes	School uniform	*Pupils can wear what they like*
Discipline	Likely to be a lot	*None*
Moral and religious instruction	Obligatory	*None*
Lessons	Obligatory	*Optional*
Teaching methods	Usually believed that teaching methods affect rate of learning	*No new teaching methods because teaching itself is not considered important*
Examination performance	12-year-olds likely to do well in handwriting, spelling, etc.	*12-year-olds much more original*
Truancy	On the increase	*None*
Relations between teachers and pupils	Teachers are usually figures of authority	*Teachers and pupils are equals*

188

B1 *(i)* picks up after
(ii) downtrodden
(iii) storm at

2 *(i)* spent time in an idle way; did nothing in particular
(ii) avoid
(iii) win outright

29 Super Race

B1 *(i)* He says he is not intending to create a master race but just a few more intelligent, creative people who otherwise would not be born.
(ii) They have turned down the request to support the sperm bank.
(iii) He sympathises with Mr Graham's approach and is disappointed at the reaction of other Nobel scientists.

D1 *Para 1* it is unlikely to add greatly to the world supply of brain-power
Para 2 the appearance of really exceptional powers remains unpredictable and highly improbable in any given instance
Para 3 environmental factors can affect measured intelligence by as much as one-fifth
Para 4 the scheme . . . present(s) no special ethical problems
Para 5 . . . may involve a very slight extra risk of miscarriage or congenital abnormality
Para 6 *(i)* mothers have not been told the identities of the donors
(ii) no one donor should be used too often
(iii) . . . indicates the kind of developments which might lead to increased concern and demands for regulation by law.

E1 *(i)* cite   *(iv)* unwitting
(ii) affords   *(v)* eminent
(iii) counselling

2 *(i)* help to explain the difficult and puzzling question of intellectual inheritance
(ii) the debate about whether heredity or the environment has more influence on human intelligence
(iii) where there is strong theoretical disagreement among academics
(iv) winning a Nobel Prize

F

The California sperm bank is unlikely to add greatly to the world supply of brain-power, <u>since</u> offspring are likely on average to be less intelligent than their parents. <u>Although</u> it is possible to cite extraordinary cases of talent being passed down from generation to generation, the appearance of really exceptional powers remains unpredictable and highly improbable in any given instance. <u>In addition,</u> environmental factors can affect measured intelligence by as much as one-fifth.

<u>But</u> if the scheme affords no promise of a team of infant sages, it seems to present no special ethical problems either. <u>However,</u> it does raise some questions which do not generally apply to artificial insemination by donor. Success in the Nobel stakes is as closely associated with advancing years as it is with intellectual eminence, and this may involve a very slight extra risk of miscarriage or congenital abnormality.

It is right that mothers should not be told the identities of the donors because of the risk of a commercial market in the genes of famous individuals becoming established. It is also right that no one donor should be used too often because of the risk of marriages between unwitting half-brothers and sisters.

In conclusion, the California experiment, though not seriously objectionable in itself, indicates the kind of developments which might lead to increased concern and demands for regulation by law.

30 Who's Afraid of the Silicon Chip?

A1 *(i)*

		Interpretations
a	The electro-technologically minded	revolutionise the whole of life
b	The uninitiated (*ie.* those who don't know about it)	*bafflement, unease, sci-fi fascination*
c	Futurologists	*the major challenge of the years 1980–2000*
d	Most of us	*substitute for fried potato*

(ii)

	Weight	Size
First Computer	*about 30 tons*	*filled a room*
Silicon Chip Computer	*a fraction of a gramme*	*much, much smaller than a finger nail*

(iii) because the silicon chip can be very cheap to manufacture in bulk
(iv) electronic word-processors
(v) it is expanding at a very fast rate
(vi) one chip can calculate more quickly than any man; computers with many chips can work at an amazing speed

(vii)

a	small firms	*will be used to do the books, i.e. keep the accounts*
b	car instruments	*will become neater and more comprehensive*
c	cameras	*will get smaller and more automated*

d	money	*will be replaced more and more by computerised accounting and debiting systems*
e	energy	*less wasted because the power systems will be better*

    (viii) the effect of automation on employment, *ie.* possible redundancies
     (ix) 'exaggerated': millions will become redundant in a short space of time
            'sober': the silicon chip will not be widely introduced quickly and will probably help to create new job possibilities

B1   *(i)* bafflement
     (ii) burgeoning
   (iii) outstrip
   (iv) comprehensive
    (v) give way to

2   *(i)* unbelievable
    (ii) for very little money
   (iii) clear, easily seen, noticeable
   (iv) very rapid; in a very short period of time; sudden

Ⓣ **C1**   *(i)* five 'standard facilities' are mentioned:
       (a) a video recorder
       (b) action replays
       (c) freezing
       (d) recording several programmes simultaneously
       (e) TV games
    (ii) a typewriter
   (iii) the electronic mail-order system
   (iv) 4 uses are mentioned:
       (a) what's on in London
       (b) booking theatre or cinema tickets
       (c) lists of second-hand cars
       (d) houses on the market
     (v) *(a)* parents with young children
       (b) disabled people
    (vi) a computerised encyclopaedia
   (vii) to receive 'letters' to be either shown on the screen or printed out on paper

Ⓣ **Gapped Tapescript**
  (1) whether you could explain
  (2) shortly will be
  (3) are likely to
  (4) you'll be able to call up
  (5) You'll have a code
  (6) what you've mentioned
  (7) this means using the home
  (8) there's going to be
  (9) you'll simply press
 (10) and you could receive it